INSIGHTS FROM PAST LIFE
AND SPIRITUAL REGRESSION

HEALING THE ETERNAL SOUL

ANDY TOMLINSON

BOOKS

WINCHESER, UK
WASHINGTON, USA

Publication by O Books; First Publication 2005, Second Publication 2008
O Books is an imprint of John Hunt Publishing Ltd., The Bothy, Deershot Lodge, Park
Lane, Ropley, Hants, SO24 0BE, UK
office1@o-books.net
www.o-books.net

Distribution in:

UK and Europe
Orca Book Services
orders@orcabookservices.co.uk
Tel: 01202 665432 Fax: 01202 666219 Int. code (44)

USA and Canada
NBN
custserv@nbnbooks.com
Tel: 1 800 462 6420 Fax: 1 800 338 4550

Australia and New Zealand
Brumby Books
sales@brumbybooks.com.au
Tel: 61 3 9761 5535 Fax: 61 3 9761 7095

Far East (offices in Singapore, Thailand, Hong Kong, Taiwan)
Pansing Distribution Pte Ltd
kemal@pansing.com
Tel: 65 6319 9939 Fax: 65 6462 5761

South Africa
Alternative Books
altbook@peterhyde.co.za
Tel: 021 447 5300 Fax: 021 447 1430

Text copyright Andy Tomlinson 2005

Design: BookDesign, London

ISBN: 1 905047 41X

A CIP catalogue record for this book is available from the British Library.

Printed in the UK by Digital Book Print Ltd.

To contact Andy Tomlinson or find out more about his work visit the website
http://www.regressionacademy.com.

Acknowledgements and Permissions

Much of the work a therapist does is confidential and not discussed outside of therapy. I am therefore grateful for the many clients who have given their permission for me to use their experiences in the case studies. Their names and personal details have been changed but the past-life and healing techniques have been carefully recorded.

Dr Peter Hardwick must be particularly thanked for reading the draft manuscript and making suggestions in describing the psycho-spiritual and esoteric concepts that are the central theme of the book. His tireless patience is warmly appreciated. In addition Dr Roger Woolger's contribution is inspirational and he needs to be thanked for the provision of reference material. Appreciation also needs to go to my fellow trainers from the European Academy of Regression Therapy including Dr Hans TenDam for his helpful suggestions. This extends to other regression therapists including those from the International Board for Regression Therapy, the International Association for Regression Research and Therapies and the International Deep Memory Association. Although there is not room to name them all particular thanks go to Ulf Parczyk, Els Geljon, Helen Holt, Diba Yilmaz and Di Griffith. In spiritual regression the members of the Michael Newton Institute need to be thanked for their contribution including Dr Michael Newton, Sally Sampson and Dr Art Roffey.

Thanks are extended to the following publishers for quoted extracts:

Shambhala Publications, Inc., Boston, www.shambhala.com, *The Tibetan book of the Dead*, translated with commentary by Francesca Fremantle and Chogyam Trungpa.

Random House Group Limited, *The Tibetan Book of Living and Dying*, by Sogyal Rinpoche, published by Rider.

University of Virginia Press, *Twenty Cases of Suggested Reincarnation*, by Dr Ian Stevenson.

Praeger Publishers, *Where Reincarnation and Biology Intersect*, by Dr Ian Stevenson.

Harper Perennial, *The Enlightened Heart*, edited by Stephen Mitchell.

The Theosophical Books, *Idyll of the White Lotus*, by Mebel Collins.

Beyond Words Publishing, *Autobiography in Five Chapters*, by Portia Nelson, quoted by Charles Whitfield in *Healing the Child Within*.

Brunner & Mazet, *The Collected Papers of Milton Erickson Vol. IV*, quoted by Yvonne Dolan in *A Path With a Heart*.

Atlantic, Daily Mail quotes.

Headline Books, *Spirit Releasement Therapy*, by William Baldwin.

Llewellyn Publications, *Life Between Lives; Hypnotherapy for Spiritual Regression*, by Michael Newton.

Michael Newton Institute, *Training Manual*.

Contents

departing for reincarnation; other spiritual activities; working in the 'eternal now'; a complete spiritual regression.

8. WORKING WITH BODY MEMORIES 153

Language of the body; exploring body memories; transforming past-life body memories; transforming current-life body memories; psychodrama; dissociation and fragmentation with trauma.

9. INTRUSIVE ENERGY 173

Background; detection; releasing spirit attachments; clearing negative intrusive energies; protection and debrief.

10. INTEGRATION 187

Integrating a past-life regression; integrating regression therapy; balancing energy and grounding; other integration activities.

11. THE INTERVIEW 201

Rapport; the objective and symptoms; boundaries and history taking; complexes to avoid with regression therapy; the adverse effect of psychotic drugs; false memories.

12. CONCLUSION 211

PROLOGUE

I sat thinking about the psychic reading I had been given. This particular medium had given me information before that had proved to be uncannily accurate. She started her reading by saying, '*The spirit that's coming through has a tremendous power and a very bright light. It says that you will be going to Brazil in six months and have two things to do. You will meet a man called 'John of God' in a large room where everyone is dressed in white. You have also been chosen to find a crystal to use with your healing that is in a cave beyond where they buried people, and you must focus on an elephant's eye to find it. These tasks are very important'*. My immediate question was to ask for more information. The only answer I got was, '*Someone will help you and you will be drawn to what they say. The information about where to go will then be given to you. The trip to Brazil will be in August and last for at least three weeks and you will travel by river. As part of your preparations you will need to take an antidote for snakebite. If you use your intuition during the journey everything will fall into place'*.

The next few months saw me checking out every new person I met to see if they had an involvement with Brazil. Finally I gave up and got on with my daily life. Three months later, Dr Art Roffey a colleague from the United States, arrived to do a talk on Shamanism. Apprenticed for several years to his Shaman mentor Don Theo Paredes[1], Art also takes trips to Peru. He asked me if I was interested in going to Peru but I replied that my interest was in Brazil. At this point he told me about Ipupiara Makunaiman,[2] commonly called Ipu. He was born in 1946 into the Ureu-eu-wau-wau (People of the Stars) tribe of the Brazilian Amazon. At that time the Ureu-eu-wau-wau had numbered 2,400, but now only 43 have survived. After a long apprenticeship as a healer and

Shaman, tribal elders urged Ipu to be educated outside his traditional ways. Following their instruction he earned a Ph.D. in Anthropology and Biology, and also became fluent in English, Spanish, Portuguese and eight indigenous South American dialects. In addition to maintaining a healing practice as a traditional Shaman, he co-foundered the Native Cultural Alliance dedicated to the preservation and sharing of native cultures and wisdom. This includes organizing trips to the Amazon. When I contacted Ipu and was told his next trip was in August, I intuitively knew that he was the guide I needed for my journey in Brazil and booked my place.

I discovered a large part of Ipu's trip was traveling by a boat that served as both the living and sleeping quarters. Our trip was along the Rio Naigro, a tributary of the Amazon. The river's acid water makes it less prone to mosquitoes than the Amazon, but my preoccupation on joining the trip was more about getting an antidote for snakebite. I was told that there was only one poisonous snake in this part of the Amazon called the coral snake. Getting a medical antidote was not a case of going to a chemist and buying it. A live snake had to be caught in its habitat under rotten logs and sent to a center that would extract the poison and prepare the antidote. Although hospitals keep the antidote for emergencies, they would be many days sailing away. I was reassured that bites from the snake were very rare.

A Shaman was on a landing to meet the boat. After the greetings I was drawn to walk into a nearby hut where some woman where weaving and another Shaman was waiting. As I walking through the door he presented me with a jar with two dead coral snakes in preserving fluid. He had been intuitively drawn to give them to me as I walked into the hut. With the help of an interpreter I found that I had been given a Shaman's healing for snakebite. It appeared that the coral snake carries the antidote in its spinal cord. To treat snakebite the Shaman applies a tourniquet to the affected limb, and if the snake is caught a sliver from the dead snake is rubbed on the wound. As the antidote from the snake's spine takes effect the red area from the bite starts to change color. In the event of the snake not being caught one of the preserved snakes is used. A fire is used to burn off the preserving fluid and the charred snake rubbed onto the wound. Through knowledge passed down over thousands of years Shamans have been using this form of healing. The second surprise was at the Shaman ceremony. When I asked if the Shaman could tell me anything about a crystal I was looking for, his translated words were, *'You heal people's souls'*. As a spiritual and past-life regression therapist the work that I do is spiritually profound but I had never thought of it in quite those words. Here was a Shaman who had lived in the middle of the jungle all his life, did not speak English and had never seen me before, but immediately understood the importance of the work that I did. Continuing he said, *'The crystal you are searching for is not in a physical form but in an etheric form. It is an energy source'*.

Towards the end of the trip our party visited a small waterfall at Iracema, on a tributary of the Amazon. To the locals the name Iracema means 'running tears from a virgin's eyes'. This sacred site has caves that have been used for healing ceremonies for over two thousand years. When I found out that these caves had also been used for burying the bones and remains of ancestors my interest picked up. At this point I had consciously convinced myself that I was still looking for a physical crystal. With a torch in my hand I explored the depths of the caves, sometimes on my knees. As I pointed the torch into the crevices I discovered they were full of large bats. Ducking my head to avoid them flying into me became a regular event as I was determined to fully explore the caves looking for anything that resembled an elephant. In some of the crevices, spiders with legs so long I couldn't see their bodies edged towards me. Finally I got to the point when I realized that I was not consciously going to find anything. After resting for a day, I wandered over to the caves and was drawn to meditate resting my hand on a spot on the cave wall. As I visualized an elephant with a crystal in its eye, a portal was opened and I experienced what can only be described as a tunnel of light leading to a mass of bright light. I felt healing coming down onto my hands. However, at this point I still did not fully understand the meaning of the event.

The final part of the trip was spent at the Casa in Abadiania, which is situated about two hours travel by car from Brasilia. Joao Teixeira de Faria, called 'John of God'[3], has made this his healing center. Hailed by some as the most miraculous healer over the last 2000 years he was reputed to heal more people in a day than an average hospital does in a month. I must be frank that I was skeptical about his work before I arrived, and also while watching videos of him doing the most amazing physical operations. This included pulling out tumors with his bare hands and scraping away a cataract with a knife without looking at what he was doing. When I entered the inner healing room of the Casa I found hundreds of people in meditation linking with the energy from the hill of quartz that the Casa is built on. Within this amazing energy I was told that the actual healing is done by spirits of light who focus the energy, in a similar way to how laser energy can be focused in eye operations in western surgery.

I talked to an Australian called Claire who was diagnosed with motor neuron disease three years ago and given six months to live by her consultant. At the first session with John of God her shakes stopped and she threw away her crutches and walked unaided. She explained that her operation had involved long-nosed scissors being pushed five inches up her nose and into her brain without medical anesthetic. As Joao twisted the scissors she felt no pain but was aware of what he was doing while her mouth filled with sinus fluid and a little blood. I found out that this type of operation

4

is done by spirits of light Joao calls 'Entities', who take over the use of his body. Miraculous physical operations like this are done before large groups to prove to doubting conscious minds the existence of spirit. I talked to several other English speakers who all told me about their personal healing. Although my doubts about his work at this point had shifted, not everyone who I talked too had been healed. This work, like all healing, has to be done within the laws of karma. Some people had been given partial or no physical healing until they had made changes in their daily life, and were told to come back at a later date for full healing.

There was also large number of healers who were going into the healing energy of the Casa and requesting help to develop their intuition or healing abilities. Sitting in meditation for up to three hours together with those coming for physical healing is an amazing spiritually uplifting experience. Those staying for a few weeks in the local hotels catering for Casa visitors can also experience being in a wonderful community. As predicated by the medium, most people wore white to show their respect for the work of the center. With up to five hundred people a day coming for healing it was hard not to be humbled by the shear magnitude of this spiritual venture. Joao has been doing this psychic surgery for 30 years and charges no fee.

Following the trip, I meet Art and told him of the journey and the healing energy source I had found. His immediate intuitive impulse was to pass to me a sacred healing artifact he had been guarding, saying it needed to go to me. Carved as a quartz figure by the Chavin people of Peru over 2000 years ago, its strong healing energy could be clearly felt. It turned out later that the Shaman from his tribe had told Ipu after I had left that I would not find a physical crystal on my trip in Brazil. I would receive it at a later time from someone who followed the spiritual healing path. Life seemed to have unfolded just as the medium and the Shaman had predicted, with everyone appearing to be players in some marvelous unfolding story, and interacting well with one another.

1

INTRODUCTION

Plunge into the vast ocean of consciousness.
Let the drop of water that is you
become a hundred mighty seas.
But do not think the drop alone becomes the ocean,
the ocean too becomes the drop.
Jelaluddin Rumi, 13th- century Sufi.

IMAGINATION — BEYOND CONVENTIONAL THINKING

How 'real' was my experience at the cave and with the healing energy used by John of God? Modern psychology has little to say about imagination, holistic perception or intuition. Most of the research and therapeutic approaches focus on the left hemisphere of the brain that is associated with rational thought, logic and verbal communication. Western culture has taught the superiority of these areas, leaving imagination to artists, musicians and writers. When experiences like mine, or past-life memories are discussed they are often dismissed as the result of imagination, meaning that they have been invented or created.

Most people when relaxed exhibit lower brain rhythms and find it easier to use their intuition and imagination, but modern psychology does not know what they are or were it comes from. In the early days of psychology Carl Jung referred to imagination as an opening to the collective unconscious. He proposed this was a storehouse of ancestral and past-life memories. Taking another approach, the psychiatrist Stanislov Grof worked with altered states of awareness. He performed clinical trials with the drug LSD and found that many of the participants spontaneously experienced previous inaccessible childhood memories, pre-birth and past-life memories. He later found that these altered states could be achieved by using deep breathing exercises rather than LSD[1]. Roberto Assagioli the founder of the therapy called psychosynthesis, and contributor to the branch of psychology called transpersonal psychology, found that altered states could be achieved through meditation[2].

Using imagination to explore other realities has been known throughout the history of mankind. The Aborigines of Australia called it the 'dreamtime'. Shamanism[3] sees no distinction between the real and the imagined. The shaman enters into a trance-like altered state of awareness, usually aided by rhythmic drumming. Shamanism spans tens of thousands of years and covers the indigenous tribes across all the continents. None of the ancient cultures left written records, but we can still learn of their practices through those who are still living and are willing to share their knowledge.

The simple truth is that for most of our time on earth, mankind has used imagination and the lower brain waves experienced in altered states of awareness, as the gateway to intuition and other realities where past lives are accessible. By sharpening our focus we are still all able to encounter these realities outside the dimensions of the physical world. Just as we can travel immediately when we use our imagination, when we tap into the memory store where our past lives are stored we can travel there instantaneously. An analogy is the command needed for a computer to access its memory. If the right command is used, the right memory can be retrieved. In the case of past-life memories the command is called a bridge and can be a guided imagery, a phrase, an emotion, or a physical sensation.

THE SUBTLE BODY – ENERGY BEYOND THE PHYSICAL

How does this work? Much of the history of physics and Western medicine has viewed the human body as a solid object. This was turned upside down when Einstein in his Theory of Relativity was able to demonstrate that the human body is simply energy, as are all things. This is how ancient traditions see the physical body, with an energy field around it called the subtle body consisting of different layers of energy each with its own 'vibrations'[4]. An analogy is ice that can be in the solid form of ice and still have water vapor around it. The difference between the ice and the water vapor is the energy it possesses. In various parts of the world the subtle body has been called chi, ki, prana, fohat, orgone, odic force and mana. It cannot easily be measured using conventional instrumentation. The Russians Krippner and Rubin reported into the phenomenon of energy around plants, animals and humans in their book *Galaxies of Life*[5]. These energy emanations were recorded in their research by a controversial quasi-photographic process called Kirlian photographs. An example was the 'phantom leaf' that proposed to show this energy.

A psychic called Barbara Brennan[6] in her book *Hands of Light* has been able to identify disease by her observations of the subtle body as accurately as the most modern medical equipment. The subtle body is credited for healing the physical body using a technique called Therapeutic Touch that is used in some hospitals in America and England. This has followed research demonstrating that the rate of healing of surgical wounds can be increased when a healer's hands are held several inches away from the physical wound[7]. Traditional methods have worked with the subtle body in healing for thousands of years. Examples are the Chinese systems of meridians using acupuncture, and more recently the Japanese energy healing called reiki. Many of the complementary and alternative therapies that are becoming increasingly popular involve working with the flow of these subtle energies around the dense physical body.

This leads on to the topic of whether any of our consciousness resides in the subtle body. Western science has nothing to say about this. The near death experience of Patrick Tierney[8] quoted in the Daily Mail is a useful area to start, because it implies that consciousness may not be tied to the physical body at all:

Patrick suffered a heart attack at the age fifty-one. At the time he was already in hospital hours after surviving a less serious heart attack earlier that day. His near-death experience occurred while he was diagnosed as clinically dead. He was oblivious to the drama going on around him as doctors at the Hillington Hospital scrambled to save his life. They succeeded by re-starting his heart with shocks from a defibrillator. He reported that it seemed as if he was walking for a long time before he came to a junction and the tunnel went off in two directions. To the left was pitch black and on his right was a very bright light. He took the right hand tunnel, which came out into a wonderful garden full of beautiful colors. He had never seen anything like it in his life. In the middle of the garden were his parents, and his mother-in-law came and joined them [they had died between 1984 and 1990, before the near-death experience]. He came to a gate and his dad told him not to go through the gate. His mother just smiled, and then he found himself back in the dark tunnel and the next thing he knew he could hear the woman calling his name. It was a nurse from the hospital.

Experiences such as these have been the source of much debate and controversy, centered on whether they are hallucinations or a glimpse of the afterlife. The most common theories supporting hallucination are that they are a physiological change caused by the dying process. They could be caused by the release of endorphins, a lack of brain oxygen, an increased level of carbon dioxide or the presence of drugs. Another explanation is that it could be a psychological phenomenon created by the patient in their hour of need.

Dr Parvia and his team from the Horizon Research Foundation in Southampton General Hospital in England worked with 63 survivors of cardiac arrest for a year. None of the subjects had any change in the blood level of oxygen, carbon dioxide, potassium or sodium. Low levels of any of these could cause hallucinations. This negated the argument that low levels of oxygen or other chemicals were the cause of the near-death experiences. They also interviewed the patients about their religious and ethical beliefs. It turned out that the seven subjects who had a near death experience were no more spiritual than the other patients.

Cardiologist Dr Pim van Lommel and his colleagues from the Rijnstate Hospital in Arnham, Holland did a more comprehensive study over 13 years. They investigated the experiences of 344 heart patients resuscitated after cardiac arrest. All had been clinically dead at some point during their treatment. 62 patients reported a near-death experience of which 41 described a tunnel, light and relatives. During their period of unconsciousness many had no electrical activity of the brain. This meant that their memory recall of the experience could not be explained by tradition scientific explanations. Follow up questions eight years later found that they had less fear of death and a more spiritual outlook on life. The results were reported in the prestigious medical journal *The Lancet*[9.] This is a nurse's account from the study:

A 44-year-old man had been taken by ambulance to the hospital during the night after being found in a meadow. He was in a deep coma and his skin was blue. Medical staff and myself carried out artificial respiration, heart massage and defibrillation, and when a tube was inserted in his mouth it was discovered he was wearing dentures. I removed the dentures and put them in a 'crash cart'. After about an hour and a half the patient had sufficient heart rhythm and blood pressure to be transferred to intensive care although he still needed artificial respiration. After about a week I met the patient on the cardiac ward. The moment he saw me he said that I knew where his dentures were, 'Yes you were there when I was brought into hospital and you took my dentures out of my mouth and put them into that cart. It had all those bottles on it and there was this sliding draw underneath and there you put my teeth'. I was especially amazed because I remembered this happening while the man was in deep coma and in the process of resuscitation. When I asked further, it appeared the patient had seen himself lying in bed from above. He also described correctly, and in detail, the small room in which he had been resuscitated as well as the appearance of those present like myself. At the time he had been very much afraid that we would stop the resuscitation and that he would die. He was deeply impressed by his experience and no longer afraid of death. Four weeks later he left hospital as a healthy man.

Near-death experiences are more common than many realize, with over 8 million Americans having experiencing one.[10] This growing evidence suggests that consciousness is a separate entity from the physical brain. Of course further large studies are needed to verify the research and bringing these new concepts into mainstream science. This is being spearheaded by an organization called the

Scientific and Medical Network, an international group based in 53 countries of 2,000 qualified scientists and doctors, psychiatrists, psychologists, therapists and other professionals. They hold conferences, publish articles and support research into new areas.

CAN SOME MEMORIES BE PAST LIVES?

We have seen how consciousness seems to be able to travel from the brain, so can it link to a past-life memory? Enter Dr Ian Stevenson, the former head of the Department of Psychiatry at the University of Virginia. He has specialized in collecting the past-life stories from children around the world by interviewing them and all the witnesses. This includes looking for inconsistency or fraud by doing follow-up visits later to check for signs of any personal gains that could account for deception. An example of one of his cases is the account of Swarnlata Mishra, born in 1948 in the Madhya district of India. This is extract from his book, *Twenty Cases Suggestive of Reincarnation*[11]:

When she was three years old, Swarnlata started having spontaneous past-life memories of being a girl called Biyi Pathak who lived in a village over 100 miles away. She recalled the details of the white house with four rooms, black doors fitted with iron bars and a stone slab floor. A girl called Biyi was later found to have lived in the house Swarnlata described, and had died nine years before Swarnlata had been born. She also identified and named several of the family and servants when she visited the house where Biyi had lived and wasn't fooled by a trick when a non-relative was introduced to her and posed as a relative of Biyi. She was even able to remember the details of the previous life when she went to a wedding and had difficulty finding a latrine. While the father did not discourage these memories, no sign of motivation of deception could be found. A total of 49 separate points were collected about Swarnlata's story and verified by at least one independent witness. None of them could be explained away except by reincarnation.

In all, Ian Stevenson and his colleagues have painstakingly collected more than 2,600 cases from a wide range of cultures and religions around the world. Many are from third-world countries where the children often live in isolated villages without media intrusion. In this type of community they are isolated from many of the variables that could be alternative explanations for reincarnation. A total of 65 fully detailed cases have been published in his books and 260 in articles.

The eminent neuro-psychiatrist Dr Brian Weiss of the University of Miami, staked his reputation and career on the publication of the case of a client who recovered rapidly when a past-life surfaced spontaneously during a hypnosis session. His book, *Many Lives Many Masters*[12] contains in-depth phenomenological account of the experiences and the reduction of the client's symptoms. The case eroded Weiss's skepticism of past lives and he concluded it didn't matter whether a person believed in reincarnation or not, they would always link to a past-life story when invited in the right way.

If consciousness can survive death and access a past-life memory, can it also link to the memories between lives? Using deep hypnosis counseling psychologist Dr Michael Newton found that these soul memories appeared to be brought to conscious awareness following a past-life regression. Calling it 'life between lives spiritual regression' he worked with thousands of clients during 30 years, publishing the research in two widely read books

Destiny of Souls[13] and *Journey of Souls*[14]. The remarkable thing is that despite dissimilar past lives, the clients would experience similar events between lives. This includes reviews of the past-life with spirit guides, planning for the next life with spirits of light called 'elders', and working with other souls in groups.

This all seems to confirm reincarnation, and a growing number a people in the Western world now believe this. A study initiated by Professor Kerkhofs at the University of Louvain in Belgium reviewed people's beliefs in reincarnation in Western Europe by using sample sizes of 1,000 in each country[15]. The average percentage of people believing in reincarnation across Europe was 22, with highs of 41 in Iceland, 36 in Switzerland and 29 percent in the UK.

A CLIENT'S EXPERIENCE OF PAST-LIFE REGRESSION

Much energy and ingenuity can be spent trying to prove or disprove the validity of a past-life memory. Just as its not necessary for a therapist who works with dreams to prove the scientific theory of dreams before they use it, the fact that a client seems to have a memory of a past-life does not require it to be proved before working with them. The first responsibility of the therapist who wishes to heal a client is to respect the integrity of the client's own inner world. Here is a case study to illustrate this:

Helen was a 35-year-old intelligent and confident single woman. She worked in industry as an accountant and was responsible for managing the business accounts of her company. She had re-occurring thoughts of, *'They are taking away my children'*, which was strange because she had never had children herself. She would get extremely angry and often tears would roll down her cheeks. Some days she was unable to work and this had been going on for about 15 years. She also had nightmares about stealing and had seen various therapists over the years but the problems had remained.

After taking her personal details the objectives for the therapy were agreed. The first was to help reduce the frequency of the obsessive thoughts about the children being taken away. The second was deal with the recurring nightmares about stealing.

Helen was asked to lie down on a therapist's couch, and repeat the phrase, 'They are taking away my children'. She spontaneously had the images of being a middle-aged mother in medieval England with no husband and living in a cottage with two children. She described wearing a long shabby brown dress with her hair tied back under a shawl, and healing people from the nearby village with herbs in return for food. Helen's voice took a different tone as she described a group of men looking like 'Quakers' who burst into her house accusing her of being a witch. The healer woman had her hands held behind her back and was taken to a river and forced to lie face down on a plank by the bank, with her hands tied under it. As the death was described Helen found it difficult to breathe and her body went rigid. Clearly in distress, she was taken through it quickly and her body visually relaxed. The healer woman had died a traumatic death by drowning tied to the plank. Her dying thoughts were, '*I'm so sorry for the children. They have taken my children from me*'.

The healer woman found it peaceful as she left her body and looked down at it tied to the plank with the Quaker men standing watching. She was asked to connect with the spirits of her children and in the dialogue was able to say sorry for leaving them. She was encouraged to check if the children understood what had happened and discovered that another family had looked after them. It was noticed that Helen still had grief in her chest and this was released when she hugged the children with the help of a cushion used as a prop. Next she was asked to connect with the spirits of the villagers. She was reluctant to meet them all without the support of others, and then reported the image of them all saying sorry. When she confronted the spirits of the Quakers the tone of Helen's voice hardened as said the words, '*You had no right to do that to me*' and was not ready to forgive.

Helen was asked to go to another past-life involving the Quakers. She spontaneously reported a pain in her shoulder and had the images of being a male thief wearing a black cloak who was trying to escape with stolen goods. The thief was riding a horse and had just been shot in the shoulder by a crowd of people chasing him. The horse turned and fell to the floor also shot by a person in the crowd. As the crowd arrived, Helen spontaneously recognized some of them as the Quakers who had drowned the healer woman in the other past-life. The thief was tied by the hands and hung.

Following his death, the thief was asked to meet the spirits of the crowd who had chased and shot him. He needed to say sorry for what he had done and promised never to steal again. Helen was asked to go back to the first past-life and could now forgive the Quakers for what they had done.

Helen recognized patterns between the past-life story and her current one. Also she recognized a pattern between the water from the drowning and a phobia of water from her current-life. When she was a child, Helen would scream when her mother tried to bath her or wash her hair in a basin of water. Another pattern was a difficulty standing up to men in authority like the Quakers.

After the therapy session Helen reported that the reoccurring nightmares of stealing and the thoughts of having her children taken away had completely stopped. Also she was no longer scared of water. A businessman had accused Helen of bumping her car into his while parking. She said, '*Previously my legs would have turned to jelly with a male figure of authority but I was able to hold my ground and tell him it was just as much his fault*'. A year later she was still a changed woman.

Had Helen remembered a past-life or had she displaced a painful childhood memory of her mother trying to wash her hair? Perhaps her psyche had somehow freely associated with a universal past memory from the English Middle Ages. All these explanations are possible. However, the important point is that by giving Helen's psyche full permission to follow its own resonance and associations she was able to come to a place of resolution and the remission of her symptoms. It is not trying to prove the truth of the story that is important in therapy as allowing the story's therapeutic power to heal.

Helen's case study illustrates how a past-life story can be allowed to emerge and be explored. The therapist does not need to have any special protocols for different types of client problems. Their role is to simply to ask questions to explore the past-life. Healing Helen's problem used reconciliation and mediation with transpersonal spiritual figures encountered in the higher realms related to her past-life. At this point the reader may wonder if this was creative visualization and dialogue, or in an altered state of awareness Helen had telepathically linked to the spirit of those souls. This will be discussed later. Whatever the reality of the experience, it seeded fresh options for her present-life, and spontaneous forgiveness in a past-life is profoundly therapeutic to a person's psyche.

The transformation of Helen's recurring obsessive thoughts after two hours of therapy was very significant. In the acclaimed book Obsessive Compulsive Disorder[16] the authors note that other therapeutic approaches only reduce obsessions rather than eliminate them, and often require up to 45 hours of therapy.

THE FOCUS OF REGRESSION THERAPY

As well as past lives, regression therapy includes the current life too. A client is guided back and encouraged to relive and resolve the conflicts from the past that have often been inaccessible to their conscious mind, yet have been influencing their mental and emotional stability. An analogy is like pulling out a thorn that has been buried deep and is causing physical discomfort. When the thorn is removed, the symptoms never return.

Traditional psychology knows that our personality is shaped by the memories of the events we experience during our current-life. Obvious ones that regression therapy can deal with are life transitions like the death of loved ones, divorce or relationship difficulties. However, early childhood events can have a significant effect. Bowlby[17] was one of the pioneers in psychology and identified that the absence of love from a parent or a consistent child minder can affect a child's ability in making affectionate bonds in later life. His research showed that this led to behavioral problems in teenage years and in later adulthood. These problems include self-harm, depression and generalized anxiety. Other powerful shaping comes from emotional trauma and memory imprinting. A traumatic event that is too large or frightening to be processed and integrated into consciousness is buried in the subconscious. This is the basis of Freud's ideas and later developed by psychologists Klein and Winnicott[18]. Many of our irrational fears and behaviors can be traced back to hidden memories in the subconscious. A simple example would be a phobia, and a more complex one post-traumatic stress.

However, our personality also appears to be shaped by past lives. Some examples from my own practice give some idea of the remarkable wide range of problems that have responded to past-life regression:

Insecurity - From being abandoned and dying in a past-life as a child.

Depression - The thought, 'It's hopeless' has originated from the past-life of a slave, and another of dying in a famine with no food.

Phobias and Irrational Fears - Unusual phobias such as fear of drowning, suffocation, fire, animals and knives.

Obsessive Thoughts - The obsession, 'I need to be clean' came from a traumatic death in the filth of the trenches of the First World War. The obsession, 'I need to check again' came from carelessness that resulted in the loss of a loved one.

Repeated Distressing Dreams - This has been caused by bleed through from a wide variety of unresolved past lives.

Guilt and Martyrdom - The thought, 'It's all my fault' has come from leading troops to their death, killing loved ones or betrayals.

Unexplainable Pains, Tensions or Numbness - Past lives that have had traumatic injuries or deaths. Examples are battle injuries to the head, chest and limbs. Throat problems from hanging or strangling, and limb pains from beatings.

Panic Attacks - Traumatic deaths involving rape, torture, interrogation and being left to die in a well.

Anger or Rage Outbursts - Loss of family and possessions by invaders, torture, betrayal and unfair expulsion from communities.

Relationships that Fall Apart Repeatedly - These often derive from lives with a betrayal by loved ones, and various perpetrator and victim roles.

Feeling Detached and Isolated from other People - Lives of being shunned by religious, village and tribal communities.

Regression therapy in line with other therapies is built on the shoulders of pioneers who have gone before and the diversity of their approaches. A history of these pioneers is shown in Appendix I, together with a summary of some of the research using regression therapy. When I entered the world of past-life regression in the 1990s I spent time working with as many of the pioneers as I could. Excellent as each was, it seemed to cover only one aspect. This book aims to bring together all these powerful healing techniques: past-life regression with hypnosis, current and past-life regression with non-hypnotic bridging techniques and spiritual regression with deep hypnosis. With its numerous case studies it will appeal to both therapists wanting to learn new techniques and to any reader interested in past lives and the fascinating soul memories between lives.

Much of the scientific effort in the West has been to master the material world. Now past-life and spiritual regression is a revolution in understanding our spiritual inner world that can lead to healing our eternal soul.

1

PAST-LIFE AND SPIRITUAL REGRESSION THEORY

*Hear me my brother, he said. There are three truths which
are absolute and which cannot be lost, but yet remain silent
for lack of speech.
The soul of man is immortal and its future is of a thing
whose growth and splendor has no limit.
The principle that gives life dwells in us is undying and
eternally beneficent. It is not heard, or seen, or smelt, but is
perceived by the man who desires perception.
Each man is his own absolute lawgiver, the dispenser of
glory or gloom to himself, his reward and his punishment.
These truths are as great as life itself, and as simple as the
simplest mind. Feed the hungry with them.*
From *The Idyll of the White Lotus,* by Mebel Collins.

Modern Western science has established that the physical world is
made up of energy. However, it has not yet provided a theory to
explain intuition, the subtle body and the non-physical dimensions
we can experience. Neither has it been able to explain people's
near-death experiences, and children's past lives that indicate
some part of consciousness exists entirely independent of the
physical body. In the absence of Western science providing an

explanation, we have to turn to other sources for a theory of past lives.

THE ANCIENT WISDOM

All the great teachers of all the major religions have communicated the same fundamental truths to different parts of the world to suit the time and culture. In their outer form many religious perspectives appear to be in conflict, but when the inner teachings of the founders are studied in depth, they have a remarkable harmony. It has been called the Ancient Wisdom and has been around for tens of thousands of years. A 'golden thread' it connects the esoteric, spiritual and indigenous teachings the world over.

For many years these teachings were not written down but passed orally by individual teachers to religious groups and secret societies such as the Kabbalists, Essenes, Sufis, Knights Templar, Rosicrucians, Freemasons and others[1]. In the last 100 years the Ancient Wisdom was written down and spread in major waves in the Western world. One was with the Theosophical Society and included authors such as C.W Leadbeater, Annie Besant and summarized by Arthur Powell in a range of books including *The Etheric Body*, *The Astral Body*, and *The Mental Body*. Other contributors have included Helena Roerich with the Agni Yoga Society. The next wave of releasing the Ancient Wisdom came from an Englishwoman, Alice Bailey, in conjunction with the Tibetan Master Djwhat Khul. A series of books were produced over the first half of the 20th- century and the Arcane School was founded to study the Ancient Wisdom.

To truly understand this new way of thinking we have to throw off our materially blinkered view that if we cannot see, touch, smell, and taste something it is not real. Rather than dogma, which requires unquestioning belief, the Ancient Wisdom is based on a series of spiritual principles that govern the universe[2]. These truths are revealed and expanded through people's experiences in their lives.

THE FIRST PRINCIPLE - MATERIAL AND SPIRITUAL DUALITY

The Law of Correspondence is the first principle. What occurs on earth also has a spiritual counterpart. This duality existed at the beginning when a single source of spirit energy and matter expanded and filled the universe. The theory of the big bang of physical matter has become widely accepted by science. The equivalent with spirit energy resulted in smaller parts of the original[3] being distributed. Specialist spirits of light use this to create new souls[4] to meet the Earth's growing population. Each individual person has a soul that is pure spirit energy and contains the memories and experiences gathered in each physical incarnation. The soul grows with each life experience until a stage is reached when reincarnation is not necessary unless it chooses to serve a higher purpose. The ultimate purpose of life is to be reunited with the spiritual source from which we came.

An application of this principal is that an energetic link called intuition exists between the physical body and the soul. In meditation, hypnosis or the altered states of awareness during a regression this link becomes easier to use. Soul memories, past lives and the ability to telepathically link to the spirit realms become more accessible.

It is also this link that carries the unresolved thoughts, emotions and body memories from the physical body at the point of death, to the soul. The medium that carries this is an energy field around the physical called the subtle body[5]. This has three different vibrating energies called the etheric, astral and mental. The etheric is immediately next to the physical one and contains the physical memories. The astral extends around the etheric and contains emotional memories, and the outer mental energy field contains thoughts.

Traditional science would suggest thoughts and emotions are located with the electrical activity in the brain. The Ancient Wisdom places them around the physical body in the subtle body. An analogy is the music from a CD. The source of the music may be contained on the CD, but the location of the music cannot be said to be in any particular place. It's a vibrating energy that is in the air all around us.

PAST-LIFE MEMORIES HELD IN OUR ENERGY FIELD

The etheric for some people is just visible as a thin gray border around the physical body. Its purpose is to link with the physical and to vitalize it. It is this energy field that is manipulated in traditional acupuncture to reduce pain. It is also the blueprint for constructing aspects of the physical body when the soul merges with the baby during incarnation. At this point physical memories from past lives are transferred. Ian Stevenson, whose research with children was discussed previously, offers many case studies that he has investigated that seem to support this. Birth marks, scars, malformed parts of the body and other physical manifestations have been found to relate to past-life deaths. A common feature of all the cases is that the body features transferred to this life are related to violent or traumatic deaths. An example is the case study of Alan Gamble of Canada from his book, *Where Reincarnation and Biology Intersect* [6]:

Alan Gamble was born with two birthmarks on his left hand and wrist. When he regressed into a past-life he began to speak about Walter and his accidental death with a gun.

26

Three years before his birth Walter Wilson, accompanied by a friend, had gone fishing off the coast of British Columbia. They were cruising near the shore in a small boat when Walter saw some mink near the water. He went to pick up his gun by the muzzle, but it slipped, hit the boards and discharged. The shot entered Walter's left hand and he bled profusely. His friend applied a crude tourniquet and turned the boat towards the nearest town, which was ten hours away. He did not know about releasing the tourniquet periodically and by the time they reached the town Walter was unconscious and suffering from gangrene. He later died in hospital. The smaller birthmark on the palm of the Alan's hand corresponded to the entry points of Walter's gunshot wound. The larger more prominent birthmark on the back of Alan's wrist corresponded to the gunshot exit wound.

Unexplainable pains and tension in this lifetime may be attributed to injuries in previous lifetimes. The memory from hanging, spears, swords, beatings and other wounds to the physical body from previous lives is imprinted onto the etheric. When a person dies this field separates from the physical body taking with it the physical memory to affect future incarnations.

The next energy field called the astral is where emotions are stored. Not normally visible with the eye, psychics report it extending a half a meter around the physical body. At death this energy field leaves the physical body and unresolved emotions are taken with it as 'frozen' memories. Fear, rage, shame, guilt, anger, sadness, hatred and despair are some of the strongest negative emotions. Had the associated issues been resolved the frozen emotional memories would not have been taken.

The mental energy field contains our spoken and unspoken thoughts. This extends up to several meters around the physical body. Even if unexpressed, our thoughts in this field have energy and are powerful. Many people will have had a time when they picked up someone else's thoughts, often without realizing it. A common example attributed to this is when we are aware someone is looking at us from behind and confirm it by turning round.

The effect of these energy fields in past-life regression can be illustrated by a client I'll call Roz. Entering therapy, she talked about the chronic pains in her joints and various parts of her body that she had experienced for most of her adult life. Despite visits to her medical doctor the pains had been diagnosed as unexplainable. She was a quite, single mother with four small children, but her voice took a different tone when she talked about her relationships with men. '*I cannot do anything*' and '*I'm powerless*', is what she reported as she talked about her domineering father, then her previous husband and after the divorce her current boyfriend:

When regressed Roz found herself as a young girl who had been abandoned as a child in Victorian England and was being brought up by nuns. She left them to work in a laundry, being treated almost as a slave because she had to stir the washing in a big heated pot for long hours for very little pay. A wealthy older man took a liking to her and they married. For the young girl it was as if her wildest dreams had been answered. However, he did not want an intimate relationship and took his frustrations of business life by beating her. She accepted her fate because she had no relatives and nowhere to go, and thought that no one would believe an uneducated girl. Finally he beat her so badly that she ended up falling down stairs, hurting her legs, arms and body. She was dragged into the cellar where she died. At the death point the pains in her body, the feelings of powerless and her dying thought, '*I cannot do anything*' went with her.

Roz was regressed back to the point in the past-life of the young girl when her husband started to hurt her. Roz's body took the posture that went with the experience as she lay on her side curled up. Her body quivered and her voice trembled as she described the beating. Using psychodrama she pushed him off, by pushing against a cushion held by the therapist. Her voice took on a new life through beating the cushion with her fists. With a sigh Roz visually relaxed and the young girl was taken to the afterlife to confront the spirit of her husband. She reported that he was ashamed, on his knees, and was asking her for forgiveness. With the new power she experienced she just felt sorry for him now.

Following the therapy Roz was able to confront her boyfriend, something she had never been able to do with men before. The pains in her joints and body that left following therapy have never returned.

The case study of Roz illustrates how the thought of, '*I cannot do anything*', the feeling of powerless and unexplainable pain in different parts of body appeared to be linked to her past-life as the Victorian girl. It was a pattern that had kept repeating itself in her current-life.

THE SECOND PRINCIPLE - KARMA

Karma is the second of the Ancient Wisdom's principles. In ancient Sanskrit it translates into 'action'. The reward of positive actions and attitudes, and a punishment of negative ones. As the Christian Bible says, 'Whatsoever a man soweth, that shall he also reap'. It can be seen as a form of cosmic accountability. We are given free will to decide how to respond to any situation and the choices we make either create or resolve karma in our life.

However, karma is more complex than this. We are given different bodies in different lives to experience both sides of a situation to learn and develop. Any karma not resolved in one lifetime is carried to another life. An example is a client that I will call Jenny:

> Jenny regressed into a past-life of a man in medieval Europe who was employed by different towns to keep order and did this by beating people. He took no notice of whether they were guilty or innocent, but used the beatings to terrorize the other town folk. Leading a group of followers he went from town to town. His reputation went ahead of him and in one town he was overpowered by the local people and beaten. He was taken up some steps to a platform in front of a large crowd and hung by his arms with shackles. Unable to look at the crowd, his death was by wooden stakes being hammered into him.
>
> Jenny was asked to go to another past-life linked to this one. She regressed into a young girl who was being beaten by cruel parents. At some point the young girl married and her husband started beating her too. She died being beaten to death with the dying thought *'I'll get my own back one day. I'll be powerful like them.'*

Jenny had experienced the abuse of power as a victim in one past-life and the abuse of power as a persecutor. Defeats, betrayals, abandonment, loss of children or loved ones, guilt and sacrifice are just a few of the karmic themes people are trying to resolve. When an understanding of both sides of the situation is understood it leads to forgiveness of others and forgiveness for our own misdemeanors. When we fail to deal appropriately with a situation, we are faced with continuing to work with the same situation or the other side of the coin. Karma allows us to learn and profit from our many lifetimes as humans to evolve to higher beings.

To break the karmic cycle we must learn to react differently to the problems placed in our path. The aim of past-life regression is to allow the larger picture to be seen thus giving more choices, more understanding and to facilitate forgiveness.

THE THIRD PRINCIPLE - REINCARNATION

Reincarnation has been an enduring world wide spiritual belief for billions of people for thousands of years. It was a global idea that sprang up independently amongst people in every continent from the Celts and Teutons of Northern Europe to the indigenous peoples of Africa, Australia and the Americas. Hundreds of millions of Hindus, Buddhists and some of the Sufi sects of Islam make it the cornerstone of their faith. Some mystic Christian sects, such as the Cathars[7] who lived in southern France and parts of Italy during the first millennium, also accepted reincarnation. However, many scholars believe written reference of reincarnation was removed from the Christian religion in AD 325 by the Roman emperor Constantine at the Council of Nicaea. This was in the interests of uniting the empire from feuding Christian factions.

An important purpose of reincarnation is to allow the soul to return to physical life and learn new answers to the old problems from past lives. Through gathering these learnings the soul becomes more spiritually aware. An example is Alice who regressed into the past-life of a bishop in medieval Europe:

The bishop was not as innocent as his followers thought. He had a secret of being in league with thieves stealing gold that he hid in the cathedral crypt. This was located under a secret slab that moved sideways. At a later point the bishop rescued a group of eight local villagers who had come to the cathedral to avoid being killed by a gang of plunderers. The bishop put them in the only safe place, which was in the crypt with the stolen gold! Although the bishop was able to stand up to the killers and turn them away, the people in the crypt had died of suffocation. He dragged the bodies out of the crypt and told the other villagers that the plunderers had killed them. Feeling bad about his deeds, the bishop then committed himself to the church and arranged for the gold to reappear and to be given to the needy.

In the spirit realms, after the death of the bishop, Alice spontaneously recalled her soul memories of reviewing the past-life with two spiritual beings. The bishop was full of remorse for what he had done. The spiritual beings pointed out that he had been loved by the local people, had stood up to the plunderers and had not intended to kill the villagers. It was only in the area of abuse of power and responsibility that he went wrong, and this would be the focus for the next life. At the end of the session Alice felt the deep peace and love from that encounter and understood why she had constantly had difficulty doing jobs that involved responsibility for other people.

Alice's experience is consistent with Michael Newton's research with the soul memories from between past lives. This is explored in more detail in chapter 7 and also in my book, *Exploring the Eternal Soul*[8]. Reincarnation is planned and the preparations include selecting a new body, parents, situation and culture for the new incarnation. Spirit guides who have been involved with this planning oversee the incarnation. They understand the soul's aims and provide assistance. Our personality is shaped during the merger of the soul and the baby's brain while it still in a malleable state in the womb. At this point the memories of past and between life memories fade, so that people have a fresh start in the new life. It is a gradual process over early childhood rather than an abrupt one, and accounts for some children having spontaneous past lives. The memories from unresolved past lives are reactivated by early childhood events, emotional encounters over the current-life and by the culture that we find ourselves in.

The Ancient Wisdom adds to the explanation of reincarnation by referring to several levels of existence called realms. It is helpful to simplify them to three; the physical, the spiritual and the divine.

The divine is the world of pure spirit or higher angelic intelligence from which all other worlds emanate. In the *Tibetan Book of Living and Dying*[9] it is called 'the pure light of the void' and 'ground luminosity' and it is the 'highest truth' in the mysterious Tao of Taoism. In Christianity it is called 'Father, Son and Holy Spirit'[10]. It is the state where people do not speak of having visions of light, because they are part of the light and there is no longer a distinction between the subject and object.

The spirit realm is where the soul resides. It is the visionary world of the shaman and the dreamtime of the aborigines. For spiritualists it is called the 'Summerland'[11]. In Buddhism this middle realm is referred to as the 'Bardo of Dharmata', the revealing of unconditional truth, and the 'Bardo of Rebirth'. It is the midway point between the physical world and the ultimate and formless reality of pure spirit. It is here that the mythological gods and visionary heavens and hells coexist in a non-spatial relationship with each other, with time having no importance.

The physical realm is the sensory world of physics that has the dimensions of time and space, and the death of the physical body. In Hindu and Buddhists teachings it is called the Samsara, which means the world of becoming. This is where samskaras, our old habits or ways of thinking from past lives are taken to be resolved.

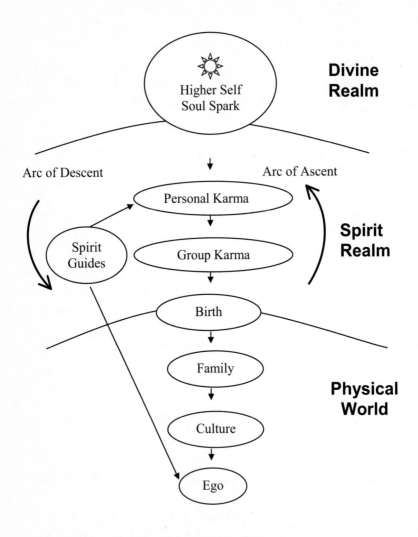

The Reincarnation Cycle.
Adapted from, *The Three Worlds and the Voyage of the Soul*
by Roger Woolger.

THE FOURTH PRINCIPLE – ATTRACTING OTHERS FOR OUR SPIRITUAL GROWTH

The Law of Attraction covers the power of our intent. An application is attracting to us those needed for our spiritual growth. An example of this is a client I'll call Sarah, who regressed into a past-life of a young woman in her twenties:

Her drunken father abused her and eventually she ran away with her brother to San Francisco to avoid him. Fortunately she found a safe place with a widow and took a job making dresses for her, and was treated as a friend. At a later point a male doctor came into her life and wanted her to leave and marry him. Unable to leave the safety of the widow, she eventually died, heartbroken and with no friends. As she moved into the spirit realms she spontaneously recalled her soul memories of reviewing the past-life with three spirits of light perceived in human form.

It's like I'm going for an interview. It's a room with windows and desk and I can see a little lady and two men sitting behind. They let me sit in a chair and are presenting themselves in a way that I can accept.
Do they talk about your past-life?
It was a very intense life. I didn't have time to stop and think or have choices. Rigid conditions were put on me to see how I would react. It was for me to learn when an opportunity came, to take it and to recognize people who I know and not question if its right and wrong. I should have gone with that man when I had the chance. Because I didn't take it there were a lot of things I didn't do and I did not fulfill myself spiritually in that life. I let my soul group and myself down.

What could you have done?

I should have gone with that man and left the widow. He was a doctor and I would have been his assistant. Not with dispensing medicine but with the care of people. I'll have to do it again. I was afraid to do it because it was not an environment I was used to. A hand reached out and I didn't take it, and the opportunity went. I've let everyone down.

What else do they say?

They say 'Do it again then'. It's as if I'm watching a video and they press pause at different times and ask me what I felt and what I should have done. It wasn't wrong to stay with the widow, but she could have found someone else. She didn't need me all the time and I would have been around anyway. I'm going to get together with my soul group and we are going to do it again. The one who was the doctor will be someone I meet in this life. I better get it right this time.

[A smile came over Sarah's face.]

The plan in Sarah's past-life had been to work with one of her soul group members who came as the doctor. This would have assisted her spiritual growth. However, she had freewill to either take the opportunity presented or not.

When new lives are planned they are progressively made more difficult but within the soul's ability to successfully achieve their karmic goals. Difficult lives can accelerate this and easier lives will extend the number of lives needed. However, the important point is that planning is needed to ensure that the issues from unresolved past lives are at the right level of difficulty. This is often done in conjunction with other souls. Thus a complex web of working together to mutually fulfill each life goal is created. We are attracted to meet these in our current-life, unaware consciously that we are setting up the conditions for repeating our karmic patterns of betrayal, abuse, loneliness, willing victim etc until the learning is complete.

COMPLEXES

A complex is the way we carry thoughts, feelings and body discomfort that seem out of context in our life. It can be called depression, anxiety, panic attacks, anger, sadness, phobias, obsessive compulsion disorder, post-traumatic stress, and so on. A common feature of a complex is that when some sort of imaginary button has been pressed the same rigid response is elicited. A depressed person may think, 'It's hopeless' and feel more depressed and have the physical symptoms of lack of energy. A person who thinks they are being controlled may get angry and lash out. Complexes produce self-defeating behaviors. Someone with difficulty in making relationships may have the thought 'I'm not good enough', which will stop them trying to make new relationships resulting in feelings of loneliness or sadness.

This wonderful poem by Porta Nelson from an *Autobiography in Five Chapters* highlights the recurring nature of the complexes we can have in our life:

I walk down the street.
There is a deep hole.
I fall in.
I am lost … I am hopeless.
It takes forever to find a way out.

I walk down the same street.
There is a deep hole in the sidewalk.
I pretend I don't see it.
I fall in again.
I can't believe I'm in the same place.

But it is my fault.
It still takes a long time to get out.

I walk down the same street.
There is a deep hole in the sidewalk.
I see it is there.
I still fall in ... it's a habit.
My eyes are open.
I know where I am.
It is my fault.
I get out immediately.

I walk down the same street.
There is a deep hole in the sidewalk.
I walk around it.

Understanding what the lesson is, absorbing it, and working out the reason for it not to be repeated is an important part of healing a complex. Another is removing the charge from it. In regression therapy they are traced back to the original source in the current or past-life. We will recall the previous case study of Roz, the abandoned Victorian child, whose current-life relationship problem originated from her beatings. Telling the story that emerges starts the process of mobilizing a person's healing resources, which can be used to transform the complex that has kept them stuck.

In Western psychology bringing to life all kinds of dreams, fantasies and images is one of the most powerful tools we have to facilitate the healing and resolution of psychological conflicts. This is expanded in Appendix I. However, compared to the great psycho-spiritual disciplines of the East it is still in its infancy with past lives. Working in the spirit realms after a past-life experience opens the person to spiritual inspiration and revelation from their higher self and spiritual teachers. From my experience of working with hundreds of clients it does not matter whether a person believes in past lives and reincarnation in order to experience them. Trying to prove that they are real would be counterproductive. I simply ask a client to stay with whatever experience they have in their inner world. Understanding the truth and the power of forgiveness can bring about their own soul healing, and transform their present-life.

SUMMARY

Until western science has an explanation for intuition, consciousness and near-death experiences, we can turn to the Ancient Wisdom. This has existed on this planet for tens of thousands of years. Through four principles it underpins the theory of past lives and the soul memories between lives. It shows how balancing karma can come from learning both sides of a situation and not repeating the old patterns. It explains how unresolved physical, emotional and thoughts are carried from one life to the next. These are the focus of release and transformation with regression therapy. Through past-life and spiritual regression, clients can see through the confusion and illusion of this life and integrate these insights into their current-life.

HEALING THE ETERNAL SOUL

40

2

STARTING A PAST-LIFE

Journeys bring power and love back into you.
If you cannot go somewhere,
move in the passageways of the self.
They are like shafts of light always changing,
and you change when you explore them.
Jelaluddin Rumi, 13th- century Sufi mystic.

All that is needed to enter a past-life is light trance aided by guided imagery, and a deeper trance for the soul memories between lives. Occasionally past-life bleed can through comes as flashes or in dreams. However, spontaneous past-life glimpses are more common with children and this has been the research area of Ian Stevenson.

Bridges provide a common way of entering past life in regression therapy. When a person talks about their complex, a thought, feeling or a body tension may emerge. This acts like an imaginary button to bring up earlier memories. A feeling of anger may bring up a memory of being ridiculed by our parents or it may bring up an image of being unjustly treated as a slave in a past-life. Tightness in the throat may bring up a past-life story of being choked or hung. When this button is found a person can move instantly to an earlier memory in their current or past-life.

HYPNOSIS

Trance is a natural state of consciousness when the mind becomes inwardly focused. An example is when someone has been so immersed in reading that they lost track of time or didn't hear their name when it was called. Another is driving a car for an extended period and later remembering little of the journey. Using hypnosis has traditionally been the approach for working with past lives. The therapist and client sit in chairs opposite each other, and the client is guided into a trance. Head and body support for the client comes from a reclining chair, although lying down on a therapist couch is useful to give full support of the body for a spiritual regression that requires up to four hours of deep trance.

Fifteen per cent of the population are highly receptive and go quickly into trance. Seventy per cent are moderately receptive, and a longer induction or repeated sessions of hypnosis are needed for them to go to deep trance. A remaining fifteen per cent of the population will only respond minimally. People go into trance quicker and deeper when they have experienced trance or altered states of awareness previously.

If a person appears nervous before starting a trance induction their worries need to be discussed and addressed. Establishing a relationship is always the first and most important consideration. Relating in a warm, understanding, caring and respectful way creates a trusting climate. Because hypnosis is a cooperative venture rather than something done to a person, it is important that time is devoted to the human relationship.

The following notes are not intended to teach hypnosis, many fine books already do this, and many readers will be experienced using hypnosis. However, it contains tips in using hypnosis for taking people into past lives, and explains how to get the best from the sample scripts in Appendix III. Many forms of trance induction are available including progressive relaxation, fractionation, confusion, sensory overload and fixation. Skilled therapists will use their preferred approach and finding a universal approach for all clients is difficult. Personally, I prefer progressive relaxation followed by guided visualization because this approach seems to cover a wider range of people. This is an example of progressive relaxation:

'and now focus of the top of your head ... let any muscle tension go ... just relax and let go ... and I wonder if the deep relaxation and restful heaviness in your forehead ... is already beginning to spread .... down across your eyes ... your face ... into your mouth .... and jaw ... through your neck ... deep restful ... heavy'

People who perceive the world through their feelings respond well to this. It also provides an opportunity for clients who have brought tension into the session to relax their body and in the process relax their mind. Many people are visual and respond well to visualization scripts. These need to totally absorb their attention:

'Imagine that you are visiting a beautiful country house ... on a warm ... sunny summer afternoon ... and you are standing on the top of a staircase ... that leads down to an entrance door ... one of those wide staircases ... and as you look down ... you can just glimpse through an open door an enchanting country garden ... it's a beautiful sunny summer afternoon.'

The therapist's voice needs to provide rhythm, and it is helpful to gradually slow down the rate of speaking during the process of induction. Subtle changes of the tone on key words like *relaxation*, *deeper* and *comfort* assist the process. The most effective way of developing the subtle tones of the voice is to produce a self-hypnosis tape and listen to it. Sometimes playing gentle background music is helpful to mask any background noises, and the most effective music has a rhythmic frequency from four to eight hertz. This is the theta frequency range of brain waves observed just before people start to drift into sleep. Many CDs made for reiki practitioners are suitable.

The symptoms of trance include a slowing down of breathing, the bottom lip starting to droop and a flattening of facial musculature. The skin of the face takes on a translucent look as blood circulation slows. Also the alpha level of dream like activity can be noticed with flickering rapid eye movements underneath closed eyelids.

The person will find they are fully absorbed in their inner world with a loss of time orientation. In this state of deep relaxation past-life memories quickly come to conscious awareness. Often only a light trance is needed and guided imagery of various types can be used. This could be crossing a bridge or going to a gate at the bottom of a garden leading to a past-life. Another example is floating in a boat to another shore to find the past-life. Alternative guided imagery can involve the client in making a selection such as being in the foyer of a large building that contains many doorways with each door leading to a past-life.

EMOTIONAL BRIDGE

When someone is asked to focus on an emotion they quickly enter into an altered state of awareness. Milton Erickson[1] referred to this as 'common everyday trance behavior'. Steven Wolinsky[2] in his book *Trances People Live* suggested that people live a large part of their lives in trance. Anxiety is an example of a trace state of the future, and guilt is an example of a trace state from the past.

An example of an emotional bridge can be illustrated with a 27-year-old client I'll call Joanne. She was a young woman who had a reoccurring emotional problem of feeling desperate which had started at the time of her third miscarriage when her boyfriend had left:

What was the worst moment for you?
I felt disappointed at the time when he left.
Are you feeling that now?
Yes.
Where about in your body do you hold those feelings?
My eyes.
Go back to the time when you first experienced these feelings.
I'm looking at the scan. I can see the baby, its little arms and legs. It's a miracle of life and now it's gone. [As Joanne said this her voice hardened with an emotional charge. After a few quiet sobs it stopped.]
What are you feeling now?
I feel desperate.
Go deeper and deeper into 'desperate' … and back to the first time you experienced it … whats happening?

Joanne regressed into a past-life of a Viking warrior fighting another clan against his wishes. The Viking took the first opportunity to leave the fight and went back to the hut where he lived with his wife. A colleague came in and told him he was needed to continue fighting. He refused because he thought it was pointless to kill brother Vikings in a feudal vendetta, better to talk out the differences. Later he was hauled in front of the Grand Council as a coward, and defended himself by saying it was wrong to take another life. His hands were tied and his mouth gagged to stop this 'dangerous' talk. He was dragged away from his family and onto a ship. Out at sea his punishment became apparent, as he was thrown overboard to drown.

When clients talk about their problem a useful question to allow buried emotions to surface is:

What was the worst moment for you?

When emotions surface asking the location of the emotion in the body can strengthen it:

Whereabouts in your body do you hold the feeling?

The emotional bridge is simply using the emotion that emerges and going to the point where the emotion was first experienced. This may be an earlier memory in the current-life or a past-life:

Go back to the time when you first experienced these feelings ... whats happening?

If a memory from this life emerges, any emotions can be released and the bridge reapplied to go to a past-life. If little emotion comes through, more probing of the client's problem will be needed. When surfacing the emotion becomes the link to the past where a similar emotion was experienced.

VERBAL BRIDGE

Language is a symbolic system to represent our ideas, thoughts and memories. The words used to describe our inner feelings and physical sensations have a special meaning. A specific phrase or word, or the tone of voice is related to an inner experience even if elegant words are not used.

A client I'll call Kirsty, was a single businesswoman who had a repeating relationship problem. During the interview when she started taking about one of her failed relationships the tone of her voice hardened as she describe it:

He wanted to go ahead with an arranged marriage with someone else, and I let the relationship continue even though I knew it was going nowhere.
What did you feel when things were not going the way you wanted?
Angry.
And what words go with that emotion?
I'm not going to put up with this. How dare you. I'm not going to be a victim. [Her voice hardened at this point]
Which words hold the most charge?
I'm not going to be a victim.
I want you to take a deep breath and repeat the words several times and see what happens.
I refuse to be a victim ... I refuse to be a victim ... I refuse to be a victim. [At this point the emotions were sounding strongly in her voice].
What are you feeling now?
Anger
Go to the point you first experienced anger. What images are coming up, the first thing that comes to your head?
Water. It's like a lake.

Kirsty went on to recount the life of a farmer's son who was tragically dragged under the water by villagers and drowned. He had previously met a rich man's daughter, and they had fallen in love but had to have secret meetings because of their social differences. Eventually they were reported to the girl's father who encouraged a group of villagers to take him away, where he was tied up in a dark barn as a deterrent to stop him from seeing her. Later he was taken outside and given a staff to defend himself because the group wanted to have sport at his expense. When they started to fight amongst them selves he managed to creep away and wade out to a boat to hide. Later he was found by the villagers and drowned.

When Kirsty repeated the phrase, *'I refuse to be a victim'* the words acted as an energy transformer to activate her repressed emotions and she quickly regressed. In a client interview when the problem is being described, it is important to listen and write down key descriptive phrases, or ones that have an emotional charge to them. Often these are phases that are repeated, or they may be accompanied with a physical movement and tightening up, or a change in breathing. The client can be asked to repeat it:

Take a deep breath and repeat the words several times and see what happens.

These phrases will always be linked to an emotion:

What are you feeling now?

Once emotions surface the previous emotional bridge can be used. Fritz Perls who established Gestalt therapy used phrases to focus on complexes and so did Morris Netherton[3] one of the founders of past-life regression. It is best when the client repeats the phrase because the manner in which they say it may have a special meaning. The phrase, 'I'm never going to say anything', may be linked to fear and a past-life of a prisoner being interrogated. The phrase, 'I'm all by myself', may be linked to sadness and a past-life of a child lost in a wood. If a phrase does not yield an emotional charge, nothing is lost. As the client's problem is discussed another phrase will appear that can be used.

PHYSICAL BRIDGE

When a client's problem is being discussed it may include symptoms of tension or pain that have no medical explanation. These physical sensations include choking, migraine, head pounding, back and stomach pains, frozen joints and chronic holding patterns. Often they can be the physical residues from past-life traumas[4].

A student on a workshop that I'll call Alan, had symptoms to illustrate this. He had a repeating pattern of tension in the throat and low energy levels:

What sensations do you have in your throat?
A hardening and a tightening.
Put all your conscious awareness on your throat. Whats happening?
It's getting tighter. I'm having problems breathing.
Adjust your body posture, arm and leg position that goes with the experience. [Alan held his hands at chest level with the palms facing outward and showed signs of distress]
I'm being starved of air.
Tell the first image that comes up?
A man has got his hands at my throat.

Alan regressed into a past-life of a Victorian servant girl being strangled to death. She had been sleeping in an upstairs room in a drinking house, which was down an alley from the big house where she worked. The master of the big house had knocked on the door of her room one night. When he entered she noticed he was wearing leather gloves and his face was expressionless, looking like a frozen mask. As he attacked and started to strangle her she experienced the hopeless of trying to resist.

The physical bridge starts by focusing on the body:

What sensations are you experiencing in your body?

Some clients are unused to describing physical sensations, so some directional questions may be necessary to help them vocalize them:

Is the sensation near the surface or deep?
Is it sharp or dull?
Is it tight or numb?

To amplify the sensations the client can be ask to adjust their posture. At a deep level of sub-consciousness they often recreate the posture of the frozen body memories from earlier events in this life or a past-life:

Adjust your body posture, arm and leg position that goes with the experience.

The client will need room to move about on a therapist couch and may need further encouragement in adjusting their posture. This could involve a whole range of positions including curling up, holding their hands over their head or clutching their stomach. Often images from the past-life come up quickly:

Tell me the first image that comes into your mind?

If a memory or past-life is not triggered it may be necessary to repeat the sequence of focusing on the body sensation, readjusting the body posture and using the 'It's as if' question. A few suggestions can often help trigger the surfacing past-life.

It's as if ... what's happening?

For tightness in the chest the answer may be; 'It's as if a tree is pinning me'; or 'it's as if a rock is crushing my chest'; or 'it's as if a rope is tied round my chest'.

BRIDGING FROM A ENERGY SCAN

A client's subtle body contains the memories of unfinished business, and an energy scan is a way of amplifying this before bridging.

A client I'll call Sue was a young graduate working professionally in a large corporation. She reported she was not in control whenever she was with her current boyfriend. This was unusual because she felt in control of all other parts of her life. She thought she had been raped by her previous boyfriend after drinking heavily but had no detailed memory of the event and obvious symptoms. All she remembered was waking up in the morning knowing something was not right. As she lay down for therapy an energy scan was used to identify the source of the problem:

> I'm going to scan your energy field to look for a blockage you have related to, 'not being in control'. With your eyes closed focus on the area around your body as my hand moves slowly several inches from your body from your toes to your head. Tell me when you are aware of a blockage, or

a lightness or heaviness … tension ... or some other body sensation ... or you may be aware of an emotion.

[The scan started]

Starting with the energy around your feet ... lower legs … knees …

[This continued on the energy field over all the parts of the body to her head. On the second scan]

I can feel tingling in my lower legs.

[The scan was held around this area]

Focus on the area that has the sensations of tingling ... Is it in one leg or both ... Over a wide area or small area.

It's my left lower leg that's tingling.

Put the whole of your conscious awareness in this area and tell me what happens?

It's more like numbness.

Adjust your body posture, arm and leg position that goes with the experience.

[Sue curled on her side with her left leg bent outwards.]

What's happening to your left leg now. It's as if … what's happening?

[Sue started to sob] *It's as if someone is holding my foot. It's John* [her ex boyfriend]. *He's holding it. Oh ... I can't get away.*

[In a flood of emotions the story emerged]

Being an analytic person who did not show her feelings, Sue was surprised at the emotions she had been holding in her body memory. No suggestion was made of where the regression would go. The physical bridge following the energy scan took her straight to the point where the complex started. In this case in was a current-life unresolved problem, but it could equally have taken her to a past-life.

Hans TenDam calls this an 'aura exploration' and asks his client to scan their own energy field. While there is merit in this approach, I find that the energy from the therapist in the scan seems to amplify and resonate these old wounds. An energy scan can also pick up other energies and this will be covered later. So for this reason it is important to make the intent clear:

I'm going to scan your energy field to look for a blockage you have related to ...

The client's focus can be directed to the area around different parts of their body during the scan. Often two or three scans will be needed as their sensitivity increases. Most therapists can detect the blockage in the energy field with their own hands, but its best to be guided by the client's feedback. In the event of multiple sensations being reported the strongest can be used. The physical bridge can be used following the energy scan.

VISUAL BRIDGE

Sometimes fragments of past lives bleed through to conscious awareness. The visual part of these fragments can be used as a direct entry into the past-life. A client I'll call Jenny had been trying to diet after becoming 30 pounds overweight. Unfortunately, whenever she tried to diet she got flashbacks of being in a concentration camp and found she had to stop. After a light progressive relaxation a visual bridge was used:

> Focus on the strongest part of your flashback. In your own time describe what is happening.
> *I'm a Jewish woman and staving.*
> What are you wearing?
> *I cotton dress, shapeless and down to the knees.*

53

What does the material feel like?
It's been roughly made and that's all I have on except boots.
Be aware of the sensations in your body.
I'm cold and I've nothing to keep out the cold. Oh, my poor body, the pain from lack of food.

Jenny went on to describe the life of a 32 year-old female prisoner in a concentration camp on the German Poland border during the Second World War. She had the job in a smaller camp that prepared the food for a larger complex. A plague of rats brought home the reality that they were breeding and eating the dead bodies from the other complex. Eventually she drifted in and out of consciousness under a blanket with a knot in her stomach from starvation. As she finally died she carried with her the memory of starvation, weakness and the cold.

Sometimes past-life fragments appear as nightmares or recurring strong dreams. Psychics, clairvoyants and people with a strongly developed intuition can often tune into past-life fragments themselves. Some clients may want to further explore a previous past-life. The simplest way in these cases is to use a light trance and ask the client to focus on the strongest part of the past-life fragment. Entering the story is often easy but it may be told in a disassociated way. In the case of Jenny she was initially asked questions to bring up the memories of body sensations to strengthen the past-life memory and then it was explored and transformed.

OVERCOMING BLOCKAGES TO ENTER A PAST-LIFE

Sometimes a blockage in a regression therapy session can be caused by the client's core complex being touched and working with body memories enables the past-life story to quickly emerge. A client I'll call Wendy said on at least three occasions 'I cannot do it', as she talked about her personal history. It seemed as if she had spent her life sabotaging all her attempts to develop her life with this negative self-talk. Now a single mum on income support she was desperate to change the direction of her life:

> As she lay down for the regression session Wendy immediately sat up saying, *'I don't think I can do it.'* She was asked to lie down and repeat the phrase and see what emotions or sensations emerged. Wendy reported a pain in her back and was asked to get into the posture to go with the experience. As Wendy held her hands together above her head she gasped, *'Oh my back, I'm not going to say anything. They're whipping me. I cannot do it. Oh help me I cannot move.'* Wendy went on to describe a past-life of being stretched by her arms while her legs were held. She had been an old plump woman who had led the local villagers against a tyrannical landowner. Even though she was tortured she could not tell them the information they wanted. After the session Wendy said, *'No wonder I don't like people trying to control me. Now I know why in this life I keep thinking I cannot do it.'*

Some people extensively use the logical part of the brain and have difficulty in using the left hemisphere where imagination and intuition are based. An overactive analytical mind can block a past-life regression. This is illustrated in the next case study of a client I'll call John:

There's nothing there, it's blocked.
Let the first image or thought come to you and say it.
Nothing is coming, it's blocked.
Open your eyes and tell me what you experienced?
Nothing happened.
Some people experience past lives like a dream. They know it's happening but it's not as clear as seeing and hearing. Sometimes people see images and sometimes the thoughts just come to them.
I don't remember dreams.
I want you to try again and just make up a story. Often they turn spontaneously into a past-life.
I'm not creative.
Have you ever made up a story to your grandchildren?
Yes.
Well do the same now. Lie back and just make up a story and see what happens?
[After a little pause] *I'm in the crows nest of a ship, its wooden and a warship is sailing towards us.*

John went on to describe being a French sailor, and a battle between a 19th- century English warship and the French ship he was on. At his death he was shot and fell from the crows nest and died on the deck below. Afterwards he said: '*I've always had a fascination for naval conflict of that period but I would never have thought of being on the French side. Also I felt a pain in my chest when I was shot before falling to my death.*'

Sometimes with this type of blockage just giving a client the permission to make up a story allows the intuition to take over. However, even before starting a past-life regression it can be mentioned that some people may find their analytical mind questioning if the story is real. They can be reminded that when they go to watch film they don't stop and discuss it, but wait to the end and then analyze it. The same can apply as the past-life story emerges. Factors that help people decide if a past-life is real include, the spontaneous and unexpected way the story emerges, emotions and body sensations that emerge linked to the past-life, and the patterns with their current-life.

SUMMARY

Those trained in hypnosis can use an induction to take a client into trance before guiding them into a past-life. Only light trance is needed and a wide range of guided imagery scripts can be used. This is often the preferred method if a client wants to experience a past-life because the hypnotic trance tends to reduce the effects of any emotions and body sensations that emerge. An active analytical mind can cause a blockage, and setting an expectation of the experience in the interview helps, as does trance depth.

In regression therapy the focus is resolving a client's problem. This will have associated symptoms of thoughts, emotions, and sometimes body tension or unexplainable pain. Any combination of these can be used as a bridge to the source of the problem that may be in the current-life or a past-life. Energy scans are a quick way of amplifying body sensations and used with a physical bridge this overcomes many blockages. When a client talks about their problem asking them to go to the worst part often amplifies the emotions as can repeating the associated phrases or linking it to a body sensation.

Inexperienced practitioners may need several attempts to find the right bridge before a client enters a past-life. If the bridge used does not link to the complex nothing is lost. The client can be asked to talk more about their problem and another bridge will appear. The important thing is not to stop or to make it an issue, but to be like a locksmith trying out different keys until the door is opened.

3

EXPLORING A PAST-LIFE

The great way has no gate and
there are a thousand paths to it.
If you pass through the barrier,
you walk the universe alone.
Wu-Men Hui-k'ai, Chinese Zen Master.

Many students new to working with past lives may think that getting a person into a past-life is all that is required. This is the easier part, the immediate task is to bring to conscious awareness the past-life as it happened and navigate it to identify the points where a traumatic event causing a complex started. It may also involve handling a spontaneous release of energy called a catharsis, from these old memories.

EMBODY THE CHARACTER AND ESTABLISH THE SCENE

When the first images of a past-life start to emerge it is important to ensure that the client is embodied in the past-life personality. Asking detailed questions about the past-life character and the clothes they are wearing can do this:

What have you got on your feet ... are they bare or do you have shoes on?

**Describe the clothes are you wearing on your body?
What does the material feel like against your skin?**

Are you carrying anything?

Are you a man or woman ... young or old?

The normal response will be in the present tense such as, 'I'm wearing a ragged dress', and 'I've nothing on my feet.' If the response is by describing a scene from a distance they are not embodied and need to be encouraged to report the story from within the person. For example, 'I can see myself standing on the edge of a cliff about to be forced off,' can be responded with, 'Allow yourself to go fully into your body ... and what happens next to you?' Alternatively they can be asked a question about body sensations:

Is it hot or cold?

Breathe in and smell the air ... tell me what you notice.

By spending time to embody the past-life character helps fully link a client to the past-life and provides a foundation for the scene to emerge:

What are you aware of around you?

Are you in the country or near some buildings? Describe it in detail.

Are you alone or with someone?

What are the other people doing?

Is it daytime or nighttime?

The therapist can be curious about investigating the situation and get as much detail as possible. The questions asked will depend on the answer to the last question. Time spent asking this type of question not only builds the context for the story but it allows time to decide if the client has entered a past-life or regressed into an earlier memory from their current-life. If the therapist is unsure they can simply ask the client.

To get the best from guiding a regression the questions need to address the past-life character in the present tense, i.e. 'What are you doing now?' or 'Little girl, what are you doing now?' It is wise to avoiding the *why* type of question because this causes the person to switch from intuitive past-life recall to right brain logical thinking. All that's needed is to simply keep the story flowing.

Questions about the details of the past-life period such as the year, the king or the local ruler are best avoided. This is not necessary for therapy, and the information may not have been known at the time. Many past lives were in indigenous tribes who had no knowledge of the year or in village communities where no one could read and write. If necessary this type of question can be asked at the end of a session when the past-life is being reviewed.

When a client gives a response, the therapist can repeat back some of their words and the way they say it. This mirroring technique keeps rapport with the client and helps keep the momentum of the story going. It is however important to listen carefully and to only use the client's words:

What clothes are you wearing?
Nothing except for an animal skin on my waist.
An animal skin ... and what color is the skin?

It's a light tan.
A light tan ... and are you a man or woman?
A man, I'm only young.
A man, only young ... and are others around you?
Yes there are men and women looking at me, they have darker skins than me.
Men and women looking ... and what else do you notice?
One of them is pointing a spear at me and shouting.

MOVING IN TIME

After embodying the character and establishing the scene, the rest of the past-life story can be gathered. Normally this will be in the direction towards the death point, but afterwards it may involve going back to gather more information as the case study of a client I'll call Maggie illustrates. She had conflict at work when she was reluctant to take responsibility for managing people. This was interfering with her growing career. She regressed into the life of a slaver on a ship in the Mediterranean Sea:

He was a large tanned man wearing white cloth over his body, a metal covered leather belt wrapped around his waist and leather sandals. Holding a whip in his hand he stood in an open topped boat with two decks of rowing slaves. The ship was transporting spices, sugar and silk across the Mediterranean. Most of the slaves were black and chained to the deck, and his job was to beat them until they rowed fast enough. He was paid a commission to get to port quickly which led to him being particularly brutal. He described the fear in the eyes of the slaves as they looked at him. Maggie's voice tone changed at this part of the scene. *'I feel hatred towards myself for what I'm doing to them,'* and a light sob emerged.

The slaver was asked to go to the next significant event and described an accidental death from taking an overdose of herbal painkiller. After leaving his body at death he looked down on the ship and watched his replacement continuing to beat the slaves. Before confronting those he had hurt in the past-life it was important to find out what had caused him to become that sort of person. He was asked to go to the first significant event in the past-life. The slaver recalled being a young boy with a big strong blacksmith as a father. The father was beating him saying, *'You have to be strong to survive in this life.'* This was his father's way of trying to toughen his son. Having gathered information on all the significant events in the past-life, the session was directed back to the spirit realms to confront the slaves he had mistreated, and his father who had mistreated him. Through the dialogue forgiveness was found and Maggie had the profound realization that being responsible for others was not a thing to avoid, but rather the mistreatment of those you are responsible for.

The entry into a past-life may be in the middle of a crisis such as being executed, choked or killing another person in a fight. Alternatively the entry may be in a calm and slow moving situation like lying in a field, walking down a path or in a family situation. As questions are asked about the situation, the story will emerge. Often it may not be clear where the story is going so the questions to be asked will be based on the responses received. When all the information about a current scene has been accumulated more about the past-life can be investigated:

What happens next?

This is a question to ask frequently because it allows the story to emerge and eventually the point where a complex started will be uncovered. If trivial information is coming up it may be time to move to another part of the past-life. This can be confirmed by asking:

Is there any thing else of significance before we move on?

Moving forward in time to another part of the past-life is like the fast-forward of a video recorder, and the client will immediately move to that point:

When I count to three I want you to go to the next significant event. 1 ... 2 ... 3 ... now tell me what's happening.

When time has been spent embodying the character it will be easier to comply with this instruction. Normally it is best to keep the flow of the story in one direction towards the death point. If the entry is near the death point, after going through this, the client can be taken back to the first significant event to open up new information:

When I count to three I want you to go back to the first significant event in this life. 1 ... 2 ... 3 ... now what's happening.

When giving time commands it is best to use a firm directive voice. Sometimes I hear a new student giving ambiguous statements such as 'Would you like to go to the next significant event,' or, 'Go to the next significant event, if you feel able.' I tell them that these types of statements should be avoided because the event might be an important part of the past-life. If firm directions are not used, that part of the past-life may not be visited and vital information will be lost. Going to the significant events enables information to be gathered about the different scenes so that the whole past-life story can be understood.

Significant events are sometimes the point where a complex started. One type of complex is called a *shutdown*. This may be when some sort of defeat has been experienced such as the body being trapped by rocks. It is often accompanied with phases such as, 'I'm never going to feel this again' or, 'It's hopeless.' It can also be recognized by a loss of vital energy when the body posture becomes rigid, or trembles or there is a change in voice tone.

Sometimes the significant event will be a *turning point* when the past-life changes completely. A child being taken away from its mother, a rich person losing all their wealth and power, or a life that has been lived with loved ones becomes a life of solitude. In the case study of Maggie it occurred when the blacksmith father beat the young boy. The turning point can be pinpointed and reviewed slowly so it is understood.

The past-life story needs to be allowed to unfold as it happens so any shut down or turning points can be noted, together with the associated past-life characters for later resolution in the spirit realms. Sometimes if the past-life entry is in the middle of a dramatic death, data gathering will be minimal. The general rule in this case is to follow the energy. If the client goes through the past-life death quickly, they can then be guided back to gather the rest of the past-life story later.

OVERCOMING DIVERSIONS

Diversions can stop a past-life fully emerging and need to be countered. This extract from a regression therapy session with a client I'll call Mary illustrates some of them. She had a busy life with a full time job as well as looking after her young children. The session was about a difficulty in confronting her husband:

Mary regressed into the past-life as a young girl dressed in a white and cream dress using a key phrase bridge, '*I'm alone and suffering.*' The young girl had muddy feet and was working hard picking up sticks and looking for berries and other food for her two-year-old brother and baby sister. Mary said softly, '*It's hard work and my poor hands hurt so much*'. The young girl had no mother or father and had to do all the work of looking after her brother and sister. The story continued, '*I'm surrounded with lots of colors. It's gone all blue and gold. It's so peaceful*'.

The inconsistency suggested Mary had skipped a trauma and was remembering an after-death memory. This was confirmed by finding that the heart of her past-life personality had stopped beating. Mary continued talking without any prompting and went into another past-life. This was as a teenage boy whose father had gone out across the water to fight and had never returned.

Mary was asked to go back to the first past-life as a young girl at the point where her hands felt sore picking up the sticks. Without any more prompting she rushed through the story of a man being behind her, hearing people from the hills laughing at her, of possibly being hurt and then seeing her body by a tree. The young girl was asked to go back to that point when she first realized a man was coming towards her and go through the events slowly. First she heard a noise behind her before starting to run. When she was asked about her feelings, Mary's voice started to tremble as she recalled the fear. The man from the hills held the young girl over a tree as her killed her. When the emotions had settled the rest of the details of her past-life and death emerged.

Mary's past-life experience illustrates some of the diversions that can stop a past-life story emerging. Dr Hans TenDam identified many of these in his book *Deep Healing*[1] and stressed the importance of spotting and countering them.

When Mary described the scene suddenly having 'lots of colors and being peaceful' she could have *jumped* from the past-life into the spirit realms and bypassed the death. Asking if her past-life personality's heart was still beating confirmed that the jump was directly to the spirit realms following the young girl's death. Sometimes a jump may be to another past-life, and its best to come back to the first one before the diversion occurred. This enables one past-life to be completed and the point of any complex resolved before working with another one.

On the count of three I want you to go to ... (the point before the jump occurred) **... 1 ... 2 ... 3... now what's happening.**

If the story suddenly goes faster or a significant event appears to be skipped, this type of diversion is called *rush*. When this occurs in an otherwise good session it indicates a threatening situation that is being finished to quickly. In Mary's past-life she rushed through the narrative of the death. This of course is useful to avoid any client discomfort from emerging emotions. In regression therapy it may be the complex related to the client's problem, so they can be guided back and the memories brought fully to conscious awareness.

If the scene suddenly goes blank it may indicate *avoidance* of a traumatic moment. Sometimes this takes the form of an inconsistency when the information from a dramatic event does not make sense. An example, if the past-life of a sailor facing drowning in a shipwreck suddenly turns into a peaceful scene. The story needs to be stopped and directed back again so the past-life can be examined in greater detail:

Go through the events slowly. What is the first thing that happens to you?

The last type of diversion is *dissociation* from a traumatic memory. This happens when the past-life is told as an observer looking down at their past-life personality or the event. If the past-life continues, the point needs to be noted for later resolution. If the past-life story starts to go vague or blank, body memories can be used to bring up the story. This is covered in more detail later. One tip is to always keep the story in the present. If a client reports, 'I'm looking down at the man being stabbed', it can be corrected and fed back as a question by saying, 'You are about to be stabbed, and what happens to you next?' Another approach is for the therapist to mirror the last words of the client's story and say, 'Take a deep intake of breath and tell me what happens next'. The act of consciously taking a deep breath often has the effect of bringing back body awareness.

CATHARSIS

A catharsis is a release of intense emotions. Western psychotherapies and therapists working with past lives have conflicting views on handling this, and this is reviewed in Appendix 1. If a spontaneous catharsis starts during a past-life regression I try to minimize it. Desensitization is a way of briefly uncovering a traumatic situation and allowing the conscious mind to digest it slowly. Many traumatic points are at the death point, so the client can be guided quickly through it to the spirit realms.

This minimizes their discomfort by reducing the level of emotion. For a spiritual regression, this approach is particularly important because an emotional release interferes with the deeper trance needed for soul memory recall.

When emotional and physical symptoms are presented for regression therapy it often indicates a complex. I'm not a believer in making a client have unnecessary discomfort, but have found that repressed and blocked emotions associated with the complex need to be released and transformed for full healing to take place. The analogy is having a thorn buried deep in the flesh. Unless its withdrawn it will continue to fester and cause discomfort. Because a catharsis is a high-energy state it can overwhelm and disorganize the logical mind. For this reason its best to keep talking to a client during a catharsis with helpful suggestions in a louder than normal voice:

Let it all out … Let the tears keep flowing.

A cathartic release goes through three phases:

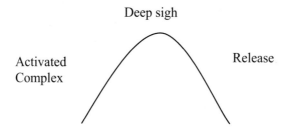

The client will come back to a normal arousal level often after a deep sigh, and then questions about the past-life can continue. In most cases the buried emotions of the complex need to be fully released before transformation can take place. It can be done quickly in one session or gradually over a number of sessions.

I prefer to discuss how to handle a catharsis with the client during the interview, and come to an agreement. A suggested discussion is, 'Sometimes the session can be intense and emotions will be released. I can try to reduce this from happening but often it will take a number of sessions to clear blocked emotions. Alternatively we can allow them to fully emerge and clear them quickly. Emotions are a strange thing. Some people pay a fortune to experience them. They call it white knuckle rides, bungee jumping or going to the cinema an having a good cry at a sad movie.' Clients who have lived with the intense negative emotions from a complex over many years are usually happy to see them leave as soon a possible.

SUMMARY

Unless the past-life entry is in the middle of a spontaneous catharsis the first priority is to fully embody the past-life with plenty of details of the clothing and what is happening around them. The actual questions will depend on the information that emerges, although the question 'What happens next' can be used often. Any mundane details can be skipped or ignored with the focus being significant events. The client's subconscious will take them to these events when directed. Normally its best to progress the past-life story in one direction towards the death point because this makes it easier for the client to understand it. The therapist needs to listen to the narrative to identify and counter any diversions. Often this involves going back to just before the diversion and going through the event slowly.

The source of a complex is often one of the significant points. One type is called a shut down. This is when the past-life character gives up a struggle such as being tapped by fallen rocks. Another type is a turning point as illustrated with the case study of Maggie the slaver. The slaver's life was turned into oppressing others after his father's beating when he was younger. These points can be pinpointed and reviewed slowly so they are understood. The information at shutdowns and turning points needs to be noted by the therapist together with the other past-life characters for later transformation.

When a spontaneous catharsis occurs the therapist needs to be the container to help the client fully release it. The level of release can be desensitized by going through that part of the past-life story quickly, particularly if it is at a death point. Normally in regression therapy a spontaneous catharsis can be allowed to fully discharge. Asking questions is not possible during a catharsis and its best to offer helpful suggestions to the client in a louder than normal voice.

4

THE PAST-LIFE DEATH

Now when the Bardo of dying dawns upon me,
I will abandon all grasping, yearning and attachment.
As I leave this compound body of flesh and blood,
I will know it to be a transitory illusion.
Padmasambhava, from the *Tibetan Book of the Dead.*

The word Bardo is the Buddhist name for the change in consciousness during the cycle of life and reincarnation. The 'Bardo of Dying and Death' is the most significant. Dying is seen as a great opportunity for people to come to terms with their whole lives, and to their own deepest truth. Sogyal Rinpoche in his book *The Tibetan Book of Living and Dying*[1] stresses the importance of clearing unfinished business and not harboring guilt, anger or bad feeling to others before death. In past-life regression, the death point always needs to be covered. By remembering the death the client will know that the life is over and often there are a lot of unresolved thoughts, emotions and body memories that need to be noted for later healing.

Many people describe their experiences of dying in a past-life with similarities to those that have survived a near-death experience. As they leave their physical body, any physical discomfort is left behind. Often they describe looking down at their body before moving to the light. In my experience about 85 per cent of past lives have unfinished business that will need to be resolved in the spirit world. In a few, some five per cent, the client will describe going up to the light without carrying any trauma. In the remaining past lives the client will report their consciousness stays with the body and is reluctance to move on. In the Shaman traditions this is called a 'lost soul part' and the Ancient Wisdom calls it an, 'earth bound spirit.'[2]

A PEACEFUL DEATH

Pleasant past lives can be a positive resource when brought to conscious attention. An example is the case study of a client I'll call Kim who regressed into a past-life of a small Arab boy playing with his friends on sand dunes:

> One of the boys threw sand in his eyes and he fell to the floor holding his face. Frightened at what they had done the boys ran off without telling any adults what had happened. Unable to see he was left all day in the blistering sun with sand in his eyes and by the time he was found he had been blinded. However, the lack of sight resulted in him developing other abilities and he became a 'seer' with psychic abilities. Unable to work he lived a simple life offering advice to the villagers and telling the children stories. The Arab was asked to go to the point just before he died. He was 80 and laying on his deathbed with some of his friends around. As he took his last breath he felt peaceful and unafraid of death, and described leaving his body and looking down at the scene below. The whole community had gathered round the house where he died with flowers and he could sense their love for him. He reported looking towards the light and allowing himself to float towards it with a deep inner peace.

Kim was allowed to stay and absorb the profound experience. She was struggling to develop her psychic abilities in her current-life and the past-life gave her a fresh enthusiasm to continue her work. Experiencing a positive past-life like this or even just touching the higher energy levels can be very profound for a person's consciousness.

UNRESOLVED TRAUMA AT DEATH

Most past lives have unfinished business and are the source of patterns repeating in the current-life. The case study of a client I'll call John illustrates this. He had a problem of speaking to groups of people. A chronic throat constriction was triggered in these situations and it became difficult for him to talk:

> John's earliest memory of the problem was when he had been asked to read the Bible at school. He had been terrified for no conscious reason, and remembered shaking and trembling while reading. Repeating a phrase from that memory, John regressed to the life of an old woman. She was dressed in rags and faced a religious persecutor dressed in a long robe with a tie at the waist. The old woman was on a raised platform surrounded with a crowd of angry shouting people and a rope was being put around her throat. Next she reported looking down at her body hanging from a post.
>
> The old woman was asked to go back to the moment just before she took her last breath and was taken through the hanging again. John found it hard to breathe and his body started to tremble. The old woman was quickly taken to the point when her heart stopped beating. Her dying thought was, '*I cannot escape.*' The events of those last few moments were of most impact. There was terror, anger, and

shame of being wrongfully accused, and the physical sensation of choking.

As the past-life was reviewed it appeared that she had been living in the country by herself when some soldiers had taken her away in a cart and left her in a dark cellar. They wanted her to sign a confession. Thinking she was going to be tortured she agreed, and was then brought in front of a tribunal of religious figures in robes on the platform surrounded by a crowd. One was questioning her and holding up the signed confession, and telling the crowd she was a witch.

After the death she was asked to meet the spirit of the religious person that had condemned her. Initially hatred was expressed for the unjust things done to her. However, through the dialogue came the realization he had only been doing what he considered his duty and was deeply sorry. Discovering this helped her to find forgiveness. Next the old woman met her friends in the crowd who did nothing to help. In the dialogue with one of them, a young man who she had healed with herbs in that life, she realized that the crowd had held him back. He was frightened and thought that if he tried to help his wife and children would be taken away. She was now able to understand.

The old woman was asked to go back to the moment just before she took her last breath, and go through the events slowly, changing them in any way needed. As John started to gasp for breath the old woman was allowed to pull away the hanging rope through the use of a prop. As the physical memory was transformed John reported that his throat felt lighter. The old woman was asked what else she wanted to do. She wanted to stand in front of the crowd but this time feeling proud and defiant.

Leaving the past-life memory, John was taken to his childhood memory of reading the Bible at school. Bringing his new experiences of escaping from the choking sensation in the past-life he found that he could remember the event now without trembling or feeling frightened. He was left with an affirmation, '*When I am with groups I will feel proud and defiant.*' Speaking to groups has not troubled John since.

After experiencing the past-life, John was allowed to change it any way he wanted. Whether the change can be described as a metaphor or a new-life experience is less important than the reality it was for John. He was in that traumatic moment again in the past-life with the rope around his neck. However, by the physical act of pulling away a towel used as a prop from his neck, he was able to go to a deeper level than words could reach and transform the physical trauma. This resonated into his current-life traumatic memory of reading at school, which cleared at the same time.

John's past-life illustrates how vital information can be lost when dissociation occurs at the death point. Going back to the point before dissociation and introducing body awareness enabled the sensation of choking, the thought, 'I cannot escape,' and the emotions of terror, anger, and shame, to surface. At death the last thoughts and emotions are extremely powerful in determining the effect on future lives. They can be magnified out of proportion and flood into later perception. In John's case they were carried into his current-life and resulted in his reaction as a child to reading to a group at school. At the point of death in a past-life, it is important to find out what these thoughts and emotions were for later resolution:

When I count to three go to the moment just before your heart stops beating for the last time ... 1 ... 2 ... 3... what's happening?

What thoughts and feelings do you die with?

A slave who was beaten all his life may think, 'It's hopeless' and take this thought into their current-life in the form of a depression. A First World War soldier fighting in the mud may die thinking, 'I want to be clean of this dirt' and become the obsessive hand washer in their current-life. The past-life character's thoughts and emotions need to be explored before or after death.

EARTHBOUND STATES

Sometimes with a traumatic past-life death the subtle body may remain earthbound and stay with the physical body. In a workshop, a student I'll call Mike, regressed into a past-life of a medieval Scottish rebel who had the tragic death of being hung, drawn and quartered:

> As a captured prisoner he was dragged on his back through cobbled streets attached to two horses by his feet. Then he was partially hung by the neck, and finally his stomach cut open. After he had been brought through the death experience, the spirit of the Scottish rebel was unable to move on. It wanted to stay with the poor hurt body. He was invited to check that his heart had stopped beating and reminded that he was dead. His spirit was still reluctant to leave the body so he was taken to a time many years after his death. All that remained were bones, so the spirit of the Scottish rebel finally acknowledged that there was nothing left to stay for and was ready to move on.

Failure of spirit to leave the body and continue the journey to the spirit realms results in some of the soul's energy, its subtle body, staying earthbound and stuck. Sometimes this can be caused by an unexpected death such as being killed from behind or from an explosion. The death may have happened too quickly for spirit to realize that the body is dead:

Do you stay with your body or can you leave it?

Often the memories will be of confusion from the last moments, so a little prompting can help connect with the memories of leaving the physical body:

Your body is dead. Check that your heart has stopped. Can you leave your physical body now?

The thoughts at the time of death often continue like a tape. The soldier may still want to stay on guard duty, or the father to stay and to try and help its children. The young child that died from a bombing may wander looking for its mother. In some cultures what happens to the body after death is important. Spirit may hang around the place of death and wait for a burial or cremation to be conducted. This can be illustrated by the case study of a client I'll call Betty who regressed into a past-life of a woman killed by her cobbler husband:

> The wife was so full of guilt about having deserted the marriage in the first place that she described herself as being full of dark energy as she left the body at death. Even after watching her husband being hung for her murder and seeing his soul going to the light she was still unable to leave to go to the spirit realms. When asked what was needed to move

on she asked for healing with light energy to remove the negative energy.

Simply by instructing the cobblers wife spirit to go to a place where she could experience this healing was she able to continue to the spirit realms:

What is it that you need in order to leave your body and go to the spirit realms?

Even after an explosion when the physical body no longer exists, the spiritual consciousness can create the illusion they are continuing to live. They become lost in a dimension in which space and time are non-existent in the sense that we know them, and stay permanently trapped and become earthbound. If the past-life has been about being a victim of the Inquisition and been 'dammed to hell' in the last moments of life, there may be a fear of leaving the body. At this point transformation is required and all that may be needed is protection on the journey. The bomb blast victim may simply want all the parts to be collected together.

SUMMARY

The thoughts, emotions or body tension at the point of death in a past-life can have a big influence in the current-life. They need to be noted for resolving later in the spirit realms. As illustrated with the case of John, the emotions of terror and the thought, 'I cannot escape from a crowd,' was carried from the witch's death into John's chronic fear of speaking in front of groups. Taking a client quickly through a traumatic death will reduce discomfort and the past-life can then be reviewed.

With some violent deaths there may be blockages and it may be necessary to repeat the death event to bring up new information until it is fully understood. After death there is a need to check that the spiritual consciousness leaves the body. Often, all that is needed is a reminder that the past-life is finished and that the physical body is dead. Occasionally the spiritual consciousness becomes earthbound as in the case of the Scottish rebel and transformation starts by asking what is needed to move to the spirit realms.

5

TRANSFORMATION IN THE SPIRIT REALMS

Die while you're alive and be absolutely dead.
Then do whatever you want, it's all good.
Bucan, 17th- century Japanese Zen Master.

The past-life and -death experience is allowed to unfold as it happened because great therapeutic value can come from understanding the truth. If a client experiences a past-life of being beaten to death the therapist does not stop them being beaten. They are allowed to experience at some level the confusion, anger, fear or other unresolved issues from the past-life that were carried into the spirit realms. Buddhists call the spirit realms the 'Bardo of Becoming' because this is where the past-life is reviewed and preparation is made for a reincarnation to resolve some of these issues. Without a physical body, time becomes of no significance and change can happen quickly. The spirit realm is also where unfinished business from a past-life is resolved.

CONFRONTING THE PAST-LIFE CHARACTERS

Understanding more about the motives of the characters from the significant events in the past-life can help in transforming unfinished business. This is achieved through guiding dialogue between them and the client. The therapist manages the process and the client manages the content.

This can be illustrated by a case study of a client I'll call Sarah. She had a chronic fear that something was going to happen to her if she went out of her house and into a crowd. Even simple things like going shopping in a supermarket meant the support of a friend and an ordeal of experiencing high levels of anxiety and panic attacks. She had first noticed this when she had visited a medieval church and her self-imposed isolation from crowds had progressively got worse. Now aged 37 she was virtually a prisoner in her own house:

Sarah regressed into the past-life of a mediaeval doctor who was thrown out of his town by the mayor after he was unable to heal the people dying of plague. As he walked slowly out of the town gates he was shunned by a crowd of townsfolk that had previously respected him in his position of doctor. The rejection left him without any sense of direction and without a job or home. He wandered Europe as a vagrant dying an early death still carrying the shame and thought, *'I cannot face them, I've let them down'*.

In the spirit realms the mediaeval doctor was allowed to meet the spirit of the mayor and express the shame of being unfairly dismissed. This was followed by, *'He has his head bent down. He was frightened of losing his job and regretted what he did. He's pitifully small now. I feel sorry for him. He can go now.'* Next came a meeting with the spirits of the townsfolk who shunned him. Initially reluctant to meet them, he required the support of a grandfather spirit. *'There are so many of them. They are telling me I was the only one who tried to do anything to help them. They don't blame me for their death, and are thanking me'*. At this point tears appeared on Sarah's eyes at the intensity of the moment. The mediaeval doctor could now find forgiveness for himself.

For Sarah this session helped her lose her fear of crowds. Over the next few months with progressively less support she was able to achieve her goal of going into a busy supermarket by herself. She said, *'It was not easy facing crowds initially, but the session has transformed my life'*.

Having working with hundreds of clients this way, including those that don't believe in past lives the process always works. In an altered state of awareness, deepened by the past-life experience, the client's psyche is fully opened to intuitive communication. To understand this it is best to think of all things as energy. With unfinished business the soul energy of the past-life characters has become attached to the soul of the client. For the medieval doctor the unfinished business involved the attached energy from the mayor and the crowd of townsfolk. While this energy stays attached the intuitive link will exist.

After the past-life death, a child can be reunited with its lost mother, a cruelly treated slave can confront the slave owner, or an abandoned prisoner can meet his family:

Go to the place in the spirit realms where ... (the other past-life character) **is and meet them.**

Once the intent is made of meeting the past-life character the client's intuition will make the link. They can then be encouraged to say or ask whatever is needed:

What do you have to say to them that you could never say in that life?

What do they say to you?

Through the dialogue comes a new conscious awareness and understanding of the motives of the other person. Working in the spirit realms calls for spontaneity and a little creativity. The therapist needs to trust his or her own intuition when identifying the approach to bring about the transformation. If they get stuck, rather than try and work it out logically, it can be left to their higher self to guide them. The more therapists practice this the more they will find it easier to work with their intuition.

These encounters transform the frozen energy of emotions and thoughts originating from the point a complex started and carried over from the past-life death.

TRANSFORMING FROZEN SADNESS AND GRIEF

Sadness and grief normally come from abandonment, or losing someone that was deeply loved. It is associated with blocked weeping, heavy breathing and depression. The strategy in the spirit realms is to reconnect with the loved ones from the past-life, which may be a husband, wife, son, daughter, mother or father. Often the client will need time just to absorb the energy of the reunion, with new information coming after the encounter:

A woman in a past-life was about to be executed and had no one to look after her baby. She had accepted her fate, but died with a deep sadness from parting with the baby. In the spirit realms she was reunited with the baby and allowed to hold it physically with the help of a cushion as a prop. The suppressed emotions turned into tears of joy as she hugged and hugged the lost baby. She was then able to ask how its life had progressed following her death.

Hugging with the arms goes deeper than words can express, and a cushion often makes a handy prop.

TRANSFORMING FROZEN GUILT

Guilt is caused when we have hurt a person or a group and have later bitterly regretted the act. Often the thoughts of 'I'm to blame', or 'I've done something awful', repeat themselves. The strategy in the spirit realms is to break the cycle of these thoughts by meeting the people involved so that the client can find new information:

> In a past-life a commander led his troops to death. At the point of death he was full of guilt about all the dead bodies around him. In the spirit realm he was asked to meet all of the troops to find out their views about their deaths. To his surprise he was not blamed. They accepted that it as part of being a soldier's life. They wanted to thank the commander for his positive acts to them while under his leadership.

If necessary the client can also be taken to another past-life when worthy deeds were performed and allowed to reflect on this.

TRANSFORMING FROZEN ANGER AND RAGE

Anger is caused when others have hurt us or we have been treated unfairly. Excessive repressed anger can turn into rage and is accompanied with a rigid upper body, and tension in the fists, arms and jaw. The other person or the group that caused the situation can be confronted in the spirit realms and the anger allowed to be expressed. Afterwards the motives of the others can be identified and processed:

> In a past-life a young farm worker was unjustly accused of stealing food and beaten to his death by a farmer. In the spirit realms he was able to confront the farmer and encouraged to express his rage physically by using his fists to hit a cushion representing the farmer.

Expressing anger by shouting or hitting often goes to a deeper level than just using talking.

TRANSFORMING FROZEN SHAME

Frozen shame is the profound humiliation felt when a person is ostracized or exiled by a group of people for some act they did. To be rejected by a community in earlier cultures was very significant because personal identity was closely linked to the group. Examples are religious orders, indigenous cultures, villages or large families. Often thoughts of, 'I cannot face them' or, 'I want to hide,' or, 'I feel awful,' are associated:

> In a past-life a nun was raped by one of the visiting priests and tried to hide the event, but when the signs of pregnancy were noticed she was expelled from the convent. She died shortly afterwards full of shame with the thought, 'I cannot face them.' In the spirit realms she was reluctant to meet the other nuns by herself, but eventually was able to face them with the support of her spirit guide. She was encouraged to let the other nuns feel telepathically what it was like to be expelled, and reported they went on their knees asking for forgiveness.

There may be reluctance to confront a group without the support of others. This support could come from past-life family members, friends, spirit guides or other transpersonal figures. Who they are is less important than the extra energy provided because shame carries with it a feeling of powerlessness:

Who do you need for support when you meet them?

TRANSFORMING FROZEN LONELINESS

Loneliness is when there has been a prolonged separation and absence of love from other people. In the spirit realms a reunion can be made with lost parents, lovers, family members, friends or others:

> A little boy in a past-life had nothing on his feet and was wearing rags. He was cold, wet, and sat begging in a shop doorway. As it got colder he could feel the cold creep into his arms and legs until they became stiff. As he died crouched in the doorway his last thought was that no one cared. In the spirit realms he had no memory of a mother or family because he had been orphaned at birth. The little boy was invited to find another past-life where he was in a loving family or community. He regressed into a past-life of a nun in a warm and peaceful garden. The nun was there to find her own inner peace in a life of solitude. Taking this knowledge back to the first past-life helped the client realized that being alone can bring inner peace.

In the above example there was no one to be reunited with, so a new experience was brought from another past-life.

TRANSFORMING FROZEN FEAR

Frozen fear is one of the strongest emotions and has its roots in a biological drive for survival. It can accompany a wide range of situations where life is threatened such as rape, torture, fighting in battles and punishment. Body memories include frozen and shallow breathing, a rigid body, a tendency to disassociate, and powerlessness. When meeting the characters involved from a past-life the support from others may be needed before the confrontation:

> In a past-life regression a young Jewish girl was having her head shaved before going to the gas chamber to meet her death. As she resisted she was kicked and beaten. At this point she gave up and was gassed shortly afterwards. In the spirit realms she was terrified of meeting the guard that had beaten her. She was joined by the spirit of her mother who had died at the same time. Now she had enough power to meet the guard.

The extra energy needed to overcome fear could be from a whole village or community, or even the therapist holding the hand of the client.

HELP FROM SPIRIT GUIDES

The client's spirit guide will have been involved with the past-life planning and can provide guidance and advice when the past-life is being reviewed. To illustrate this I'll use the case study of a client I'll call Anne. She was a woman in her thirties who had a dependant relationship with a dominating mother. Having worked all her life in the mother's business she was low in self-confidence, and unable to develop deep relationships thinking others always talked about her and hated her:

> She regressed into the life of a mother having her children taken away by North American pilgrims. They told her that with the absence of a husband she was a bad mother. Her small cabin in the forest was set on fire and afterwards she sat down by herself reflecting on the events. As an outsider none of the pilgrims had listened to her pleas to keep the children. She decided to try and reason with the pilgrim elders from the community and even beg with them if necessary to get her children back. When she reached the settlement the pilgrims ignored her and some even laughed. The pilgrim elders held all the power in the community and told her she could only have the children back if she conformed. She would have to dress correctly, take the role of a humble pilgrim woman and be subservient to the men for a test period of a year. Afterwards the children would be returned.

> She complied but felt dreadful because no one in the community would have anything to do with her. Some of the children shouted abuse and some threw stones, but she was determined to accept whatever happened to get her children back. After a year she was devastated when the pilgrim elders said the children were happy with the family looking after them and did not want to come back. She felt grief and loss and there was nothing she could do. As she grew old in the settlement she became mad and had to be chained by the wrist in a room with straw on the floor. She became thin, filthy, and her hair tatty. Her dying feeling was sadness and a longing for her children.

> In the spirit realms the pilgrim mother was reluctant to meet the children because she thought they would be

ashamed of her, and reluctant to meet the pilgrim elders because she could not trust them. Her spirit guide was requested and in the dialogue she found the children had grown up and had their own families in the settlement. They were too young at the time to remember much of her or the events. At this point the pilgrim mother was able to meet the spirit of her children and tell them how much she loved them. With the help of a cushion as a prop she was able to hug them, and in the emotional encounter the sadness and longing for the children was released. With the support of her spirit guide she was then able to confront the pilgrim elders and through the dialogue she reported that they had bowed their heads and one was pleading for forgiveness. She was now able to let them go.

Introducing her spirit guide into the dialogue overcame a blockage and enabled the spirit of the pilgrim mother to be eventually reunited with her children. Anne was able to integrate the session into her current-life and into her relationship with her domineering mother. She was able to stand up to her for the first time and moved to London into a new career.

While working in the spirit realms a therapist may get to a point when they are unsure of what to do next, or the client may appear stuck in moving towards forgiveness. Someone who has been in conflict with another soul for many lifetimes without reconciliation may have difficulty finding forgiveness. Introducing a spirit guide[1] will give a broader vision or a deep spiritual insight:

Ask your spirit guide to come to you ... what advice is offered?

In an altered state of awareness the client will find they are able to intuitively communicate with them. Sometimes whole chains of lifetimes and karmic patterns become clear and obvious. In many cases the victim has been the persecutor, the wife beater has been the abused wife. They may be shown the higher spiritual levels and experience the peace and tranquility, which can be very healing to the soul.

REACHING FORGIVENESS

The act of forgiving another person or to forgive our self is enormously powerful. True forgiveness involves unreservedly forgiving without any residual guilt or blame. This wonderful true story sums up the power of forgiveness:

John was a prisoner of the Japanese during the Second World War. He had been asked to hide a map by a fellow prisoner, but unfortunately the map was found. For three whole days a Japanese Officer who wanted to know about his planned escape tortured him. He was unable to answer the questions and was eventually left for dead slumped on the floor. His colleagues helped him recover and amazingly he survived the war and was eventually released.

Back in England he was full of hatred towards the Japanese for what they had done. He found that he could no longer hold down a job, and his relationship with his wife suffered and eventually she left him. He turned to drink and wondered the streets destitute. One day quite by chance he met one of his fellow prisoners from the camp and was told about a prisoner reunion. With help he was able to attend. What he did not know was that some of the Japanese soldiers had also been invited, and John found himself face to face with the Japanese officer who had brutally tortured him. The officer immediately recognized him and came to him. He explained that if he had not interrogated him someone else would have done it and he would have been shot for disobeying an order. The pain of his guilt had stayed with him every day since the event and he begged for forgiveness. John spontaneously found himself hugging the Japanese office and was able to forgive him. Afterwards John found that his life changed. He got a job, a new relationship and had let go of his hatred for the Japanese.

In past lives forgiveness normally comes after the confrontation in the spirit realms when the motivation, intentions and actions of the others are understood. Care is needed in situations when forgiveness seems to come too quickly because it may not be true forgiveness. A public humiliation deprives the person of power and by being able to face the crowd and say the words that could never be said at the time is very empowering. Even if a client says there is forgiveness, it is still useful to meet the past-life characters particularly from shutdowns and turning points.

Discovering forgiveness spontaneously through the dialogue is a powerful way to get meaningful completion. The following question is an example of what can asked:

Do you need any more information ... or can you let them go?

Sometimes the other past-life character may not show signs of forgiveness when the client has been a victim. Often this hampers the forgiveness process and two useful suggestions are:

Telepathically show your hurt to them ... what happens now?

Send a small fragment of love energy to them... what happens now?

Spontaneous forgiveness signals the end of the unfinished business. Often words like, 'I understand now' or, 'I can let them go now' indicates forgiveness.

ENERGY SCANNING FOR UNFINISHED BUSINESS

Just as an energy scan can be used to identify unfinished business before a regression, it can also be used to spot any remaining unfinished business at the end of a session. A case study example is a client I'll call Maggie who was in a long-term abusive relationship with an alcoholic husband. Although she believed that it was her task to help him, she still looked for a reason to leave:

> She regressed into the past-life of a sick young woman lying in bed. A noise was heard outside the house and venturing out she found a red haired man on a horse. He confronted her by shouting and holding a sword in his hand. Fearing for her life she started to run away, but he quickly caught up with her and dragged her along the ground by her hair. Next she felt the hooves of the horse trampling on her and she died face down in the dirt.
>
> As the past-life was reviewed it appeared that her mother had died when she was born and she had grown up isolated from the local villagers deliberately by her father. When he became ill she looked after him. Not having any worldly knowledge other than living in the house by herself she had nowhere to go after her father's death. Until the encounter with the red haired man she had survived on money that her father had left her.
>
> In the spirit realms the young woman was asked to meet the spirit of her father, and discovered he thought she was special and different from the villagers because of her

95

psychic visions. He was concerned that if the villagers had found out they would not have understood and would have harmed her. The young woman was ready to let him go.

Next she confronted the red haired man to find out why she was killed. In the dialogue she found out he was drunk and had thought she was evil because of her visions. The encounter had got out of hand and he now regretted his actions. It appeared that this new information would be enough.

Maggie's body was scanned for any unfinished business from the past-life. She identified anger and a tension in her head towards the red haired man, who she also intuitively recognized as her abusive husband in this life. She was taken to the point before he killed he and encouraged to express the anger and shouted, *'I hate you for what you did'*. Energy shifted and another body scan of Maggie's body confirmed that all the tension had been released. At this point the young woman felt sorry for the red haired man and was ready to forgive him.

Maggie recognized many patterns from the past-life working out in her current live. The most profound was the pattern between the red haired man and her abusive husband. She was able to take the step that had been too difficult in the past and find her freedom by finishing the abusive relationship.

Maggie's past-life illustrates how energy scanning can be used to quickly identify any remaining frozen energy from the past-life. This sort of scanning is similar to the energy scanning bridge. The client's energy field is scanned with the therapist's hands several inches from the physical body, from the toes to the head. It is important to make the intent clear that the scan is for energy blockages still remaining from the past-life. If the client reports an emotion or a discomfort from some part of the body it can be used as a bridge to go back to the point in the past-life when it was created. The residual frozen energy can then be released and transformed.

> **Focus on ...** (the body sensation or emotion) **and when I count to three, go to the point just before it happened ... 1 ... 2 ... 3 ... now what's happening?**

It may be a catharsis never released or a body memory still needing transformation. Alternatively it may be a current-life memory still resonating with the past-life complex. These need to be explored and transformed, and the techniques are covered in later chapters.

SUMMARY

The past-life and -death experience is allowed to unfold as it happened because great therapeutic value can come from understanding the truth. The client is encouraged to meet all the characters from the significant events, particularly shut downs or turning points when a complex started. They can be allowed to say whatever they want and the answers come intuitively. This brings to conscious awareness the motives of the other person, new insights and understanding.

Spontaneous forgiveness to others and oneself at the end of a confrontation is powerful and can bring an end to unfinished business. Sometimes clients simply say its finished or they can let the others go. If a therapist has problems guiding the process of spiritual transformation the client's spirit guide can be requested to give new spiritual insights. An energy scan will confirm that nothing has been missed.

6

BETWEEN LIVES SPIRITUAL REGRESSION

Leave the familiar for a while
and let your senses and bodies stretch out.
Greet yourself in your thousand other forms
as you mount the hidden tide and travel back home.
Mohammad Hafiz, 14th- century Persian.

INTRODUCTION

In a past-life regression, the spirit realms are experienced in the *eternal now*. This is an altered state of awareness in which the client finds it easy to communicate intuitively with the souls of the other past-life characters and their spirit guide. I have illustrated through case studies how interactive discussion can take place giving insights and transformation from these encounters. Michael Newton took a different approach in the spirit realms by allowing clients to recall their soul memories. His book *Life between Lives Hypnotherapy for Spiritual Regression*[1] highlights his techniques. This and the work of the association he established called the Michael Newton Institute[2] has been the basis for this chapter. I have adapted and introduced changes that I consider simplifies the process. A spiritual regression enables people to experience how their own soul prepared for the next life. They can experience the multi-dimensional spiritual activities of the soul and answer at a profound level the questions, 'Who am I?' and 'Why am I here?'

After death a person's soul energy returns to the spirit realms for a time for reflection and for meeting its soul group. These are other souls that have been assigned to work together and often jointly reincarnate together on some meaningful task. A highlight during some part of the time in the spirit realms is to meet the elders. These are souls who have attained a level of experience and wisdom that not does require them to physically reincarnate. They review the progress of the soul before them and can replay any of its past lives and discuss aspects, until the soul understands what will be expected in the next life. Achieved with love, compassion, and the participation of the soul, it leads to the next physical incarnation having a purpose. Goals are set based on the patterns from previous karmic experiences, and new lessons are agreed between the soul, its spirit guide and the elders. Sometimes clients report an intense spiritual presence behind or above the elders. The energy is too strong and subtle for them to explore, but it is thought that the elders work at higher vibration of energy to tune into this divine source.

PREPARATION

An important part of the preparation for a spiritual regression is to ensure that deep hypnosis can be experienced without problems. 70 per cent of the population are only moderately receptive and 15 per cent are non responsive. I supply a self-hypnosis CD so that the client can get used to my voice and the induction script as well as experience hypnosis frequently. The more times people experience trance, the deeper they can go. Rather than have the disappointment of not going into deep hypnosis during the spiritual regression it is far better to resolve this problem beforehand.

For those who have not experienced a past-life or hypnosis, a separate past-life regression using hypnosis can be arranged before the spiritual regression. This is particularly useful for the analytical client so that they can get used to the intuitive information flow from a past life first. A separate regression therapy can also clear blocked emotions that would otherwise interfere with the spiritual regression.

The preparation also includes the client thinking about the spiritual objectives for their regression. Typically people want to understand the purpose for their current-life, their karmic and spiritual progress or just to experience their soul journey in the spirit realms. I always ask for a list of the names of significant people from the client's current-life. Typically this list can be up to eight key people who have had a positive or negative impact, together with their relationship and three adjectives to describe each of them. An example is; mother - loving, controlling, and remote. Often the souls of these people are recognized during the regression and it helps the therapist understand who they are.

I also point out that the client's experiences may be different from what they may have read on the subject. No two sessions are the same because each soul is unique and the conscious mind interprets its stored memories in different ways. Some sessions are in great detail and some less so, some with visual experiences and some without. I advise the client to be open to the universe and allow the experience to come to them in whatever form is appropriate. Subconscious soul memories once tapped into will always reveal the truth.

I also explain what will happen in hypnosis. Initially they will be helped to relax and then visualizations will be used to take them into deeper levels of relaxation. Discussing this with the client and asking if they have any preferences for the induction gives them an element of control that will assist in deepening the hypnosis.

The sessions are between three and four hours in duration so it is important for the client to be fully supported in a reclining armchair or lying on a therapist's couch. In deep trance changing physical position to relieve any pressure is not possible, so being comfortable is important. A blanket over the body will help to protect against cold when the blood circulation slows in trance.

Time needs to be set aside by the client after the session for a stress-free period to reflect on the experience. The sessions are also intense for the therapist because during most of the spiritual regression they will be intuitively linked with the client and various spiritual helpers. To avoid 'therapist burn out' I recommended only one spiritual regression is planned a day. I personally feel drained after a session and need to ground myself by spending time going for a walk or working in the garden.

The information from the regression needs to be recorded because many clients get new insights each time they listen to the recording. It is also very personal, so I recommend that any friends or spouses avoid attending the regression. They may be part of the karmic pattern that is revealed in the session. Checks need to be made for contra indicators particularly medication, recreational drugs or emotional upheavals. The spiritual regression is not intended to release and clear complexes.

DEEPENING THE HYPNOSIS

For a spiritual regression, clients need to be in deep hypnosis. A suggested hypnosis script for a spiritual regression is shown in Appendix III. Up to 45 minutes of trance induction and deepening may be needed to take a person to the deep levels where they have free access to the detailed information of their soul memories. Depth testing is an inexact science. Scales like *LeCron-Bordeaux* and *Arons* have their merit but they do not apply in all cases to all clients. In deep hypnosis, blood circulation slows and this can be observed by the color of the skin tone of the face becoming paler. Breathing will be very shallow, the client's body movements will cease and there will be an increasing delay in responding to questions or physical signaling. The bottom lip will start to droop and there may be a flattening of the facial musculature. Often there will be involuntary swallowing in the throat.

I prefer to check on trance depth using finger movement indication. Depth of trance can also be assessed by the delay in response and slow jerky movement of the finger. Also in deeper trance the command will be interpreted literally so the finger will continue to rise until acknowledged:

'Imagine a scale … with 10 representing wide-awake … and 1 representing the deepest relaxation you can possibly go too … and as I count down the scale from 10 to 1 …. let the finger on your hand lift to indicate your depth of trance ... 10 … 9… 8… 7…' and so on.
Wait for a finger to lift, 'Good'

Depending on the feedback further deepening can use stairs or 'dropping the numbers' or similar techniques. Sometimes for light trance levels the client may need to be brought back to full awareness to find out what they were experiencing, and then alternative trance approaches used. Failure to respond to a finger signal request may be because the client is so deep in trance that the response has been too small to notice.

Michael Newton's contribution to deepening has been with age regression. This is a variation of the stair-deepening method. The client is asked to imagine moving down a stairway into their childhood with a suggestion they will go deeper with each step of the stairs. It further deepens the trance and allows for a final trance assessment. The assessment is made by the qualities on the voice and the access to memories thought beyond conscious recall.

Some of the trance factors are an increased delay in answering questions, a quiet voice and answering questions literally. They should be replying as if they are the young person again and recalling the details of their past without having to consciously strain to remember. Of course only neutral or pleasant memories should be explored. If a trauma or emotional problem has been experienced at any age then that age should be avoided with this technique.

The client's experience can be anchored at the deepest part of trance induction with a phrase. At any future point in the regression this phrase can be used for deepening. Alternatively the anchor can be going to a special place, a snap of the fingers or by touching an arm or the forehead. When clients talk they often drift to lighter levels of trance and then the anchor can be used. In addition they can be asked to stay focused on the visualization imagery of the past-life or spiritual regression. Focusing on their inner world for a while without talking deepens the experience:

'Be aware of all the details you see or experience. When I ask you to talk again tell me about them'.

The anchor and visualization may sometimes have to be repeated all the way through a past-life and sometimes in the spirit realms. However, by initially investing the time in getting the right level of trance, the trance depth will be maintained while talking.

The use of deep hypnosis often makes it easier to reduce spontaneous negative emotions that may interfere with entering a spiritual regression. I remember one client recalling a past-life of a prisoner during the time of the Spanish Inquisition. As he was tortured to confess, he was able to describe his fingernails being removed one by one with the minimum of discomfort:

'I want you to visualize having a powerful golden shield of light around you, from head to toe giving you light and power. Any painful feeling from the past will bounce off your shield of protective light'.

On a practical matter, a client will sometimes need to go to the toilet. They will always find they can express this need even in the deepest of trace. Rather than being brought fully out of trance, the client can be brought to a level of awareness that will enable them to walk to the toilet with a little support:

'You will be brought to a lighter level of trance so that you can go to the toilet. I'll escort you and when you lay down again you will be able to immediately go into deeper trance and continue your soul memories at the point you left them. Counting from three to one and on the count of one being able to walk to the toilet ...'

On their return the client will find it quick to slip into deep trance again and continue the regression at the point they left it.

ENTRY TO THE SPIRIT REALMS

The entry point to a spiritual regression is from the death in the past-life. A case study to illustrate this is a client I'll call Oscar. He regressed into a past-life of being a big strong blacksmith wearing armor. He had been joined by his fellow villagers to fight invading Romans, and was eventually overwhelmed and found himself with his hands tied in a clearing. He could see the back of one of his colleagues kneeling with his hands tied behind his back and his head bent down. He watched as the head was cut off and the body thrown onto a big fire. The blacksmith avoided looking at the executioner as he grimly went to the same death:

I can just hear the swish of the knife. [pause] *I cannot hear anything any more. I can't see anything.*

Check your heart has stopped beating. Do you stay with the body or move on?

I stay. Oh, I can now see a whole battlefield, horses and people and there is a whole line of captured soldiers waiting to meet their fate.

Do you feel drawn to stay with this battlefield or can you move on now?

There's nothing left for me.

Are you carrying any emotions or feelings with you?

It's still with me. It's just a waste to be defeated. I could have fought so many more battles. It's so unjust.

Are you staying or move away?

Moving away.

Is something pulling you or are you doing it yourself?

[pause] *A bit of both.*

Are you looking ahead in the direction you are going or backwards at the Earth?

Going through the clouds. Very fast.

Tell me what you notice?

Just one bright light, it's huge. It's all around me. It's sort of white and yellow light.

Do you recognize what this light is?

No. [pause] *It feels like I'm back home.*

What happens next?

[long pause] *There's a figure coming towards me.*

Look at the figure and describe it. Is it in energy form or human form?

It's difficult to describe. It's golden yellow white appearance. It's got sort of arms and legs but whispery.

Simmering, and it's come to greet me. Not as bright as the light all around.

The energy that's come to meet you, do you recognize it?

It takes on the appearance of a woman. [surprised voice] *It's my guide.*

What's the name of your guide?

It beings with a Z ... Z.

Try pronouncing it?

Zenestra.

What was the energy that first experienced before your guide came?

It was just a bright light. Zenestra has just embraced me with a look of relief, longing, all put into one.

Do you review that life?

Not yet, but all the feeling of such waste and futility has just gone. I don't feel it any more. I feel like I'm back to normal.

Is this some sort of healing you had?

Yes.

This part of Oscar's spiritual regression followed his past-life death as a blacksmith and the cross over into the spirit realms. The normal entry point to a spiritual regression is from the death in the client's *last* past-life. Sometimes however their higher mind selects another one if it is more relevant. In the case of Oscar he went back to a past-life in Roman times. I try to navigate the past-life and get to the death point reasonably quickly because the past-life will be fully reviewed in the spirit realms, normally with the spirit guide. It also gives more time to work with the soul memories between lives. Any spontaneous catharsis should be unlikely because of the deep hypnosis, but if it does occur at the past-life death the client can be quickly brought through the death to reduce any interruption with the entry to the spirit realms.

Some clients remember looking backward as they leave Earth, while others look forward. Oscar found he was observing the battlefield and was still left with the emotions and thoughts of the injustice done to him. Some clients have memories of the difficulty they experienced in adjusting to being a soul again or are in a state of confusion following a sudden death. So directive questions are more useful to guide them a little quicker through this difficult part of the journey:

Go to the point when you leave your body. Do you leave by yourself or feel any sort of pull?

Are you looking behind at the Earth as you leave or in front of you?

After energy healing in spirit realms the soul memories become clearer and open-ended questions can be asked routinely. There may be a delay in the answer to a question, so when waiting for a reply it is best to be patient and not ask the next question until the first has been answered.

All clients report at some point seeing lights. These are welcoming souls who help in the transition to the spirit realms. There is no need to gather great detail at this point. A larger single light is usually the spirit guide:

As you get closer do you see a single light or a number of light in the distance?

Does any light drift close to you or do you go towards it?

If the past-life death has been traumatic, clients will report going to a place of energy healing. Sometimes they may say they have gone to a crystalline enclosure and their energies are being balanced. Oscar was just aware briefly of energy surrounding him and his negative thoughts and feeling about the past-life disappearing. This has been called rejuvenation energy and its purpose is to reduce the dense lower negative energy or add new energy before meeting other souls in the spirit realms. The traumatic memories are not lost, just the dense energy from them removed. Through this process the soul energy vibrations are increased so they can safely meet other souls of their true vibration:

Describe the place that you have been drawn to go to?

Is any energy being added or taken away from you?

Experiencing this healing has a profound effect on the conscious mind and I have found that in some cases it may take several minutes until they say it is complete. Some therapists ask the client to move to the point when its finished so that the story can continue. My preference is to allow the client to explore the experience fully. Often they report their soul energy changing color, or several spirits of light surround them using different colored healing energies. Sometimes I have been intuitively drawn to place my hands on the client's energy field and channel energy healing. It allows the experience to be felt in their current physical body too and also deepens the client's trance before moving on:

Look at the color of your energy field and tell me the changes from when you entered?

Provided trance depth has been previously achieved this part is normally straightforward. If the client reports blackness, the therapist can be a little more directive and ask them to imagine an unseen hand directing them to a beautiful spiritual world.

Alternatively they can be asked to go to the place where their spirit guide is, and bypass the entry to the spirit realms. If the client reports difficulty remembering anything after the past-life death it may indicate that the trance depth is not deep enough. Occasionally the spirit guide may block access to the soul memories. This generally means that the person has not progressed to the life stage when this information can be made available. Perhaps they are about to make a major decision in their life and the guide does not want to interfere with freewill and the amnesia block needs to stay in place. All that can be done is to bring the client out of trance and discuss what happened. It is important to stress that they are not failures because there is a reason for what happened. Alternatively if it has been agreed before with the client, that past life can be further explored and transformed,

PAST-LIFE REVIEW WITH THE SPIRIT GUIDE

The past-life review is normally done shortly after the energy healing, and can be a solitary exercise or done with other spirits of light, usually the spirit guide. In the case study of a client I'll call Heather it covers the review with her spirit guide. She regressed into the past-life of a 50-year-old female Victorian teacher who was single and went on to become a governess of rich family. She taught their big family of children, and died peacefully and happy at having found such a loving family. With them gathered around her bed, she found it hard to breath and quietly died:

I'm floating up.
Do you look upwards or down?

I'm looking down. I see Mary and Charles and the doctor tendering to me as I go higher and higher. I think they are crying.

Are you able to leave them and continue your journey?

Yes.

Can you see any lights in the distance?

It just appears to be brighter ahead. Yes, very bright.

Do you head for it?

Yes.

Tell me what happens when you get to the light?

[Long Pause]

It feels as if I'm just in the light.

Describe what it's like?

It's ... it feels very safe ...[Long pause] I feel a presence. It's hard to put into words.

Do you recognize the presence; a relative or guide or teacher?

I just feel a presence, I cannot describe it.

Do you know who this presence is?

I think it's a guide.

What happens?

I get a feeling we are going somewhere. Floating along.

What happens next?

I'm in a tunnel and floating behind. I feel perfectly fine. I'm being taken. I'm their now and it feels crowded. Lots of energy forms. They are in groups.

How many different groups are there?

Twenty or more, it's very big this place.

Count all the energy forms?

Uh. I want to say 693. [pause] I'm in a smaller room now. I'm with my guide.

Anyone else?

No.

Is the guide in energy or human form?

Energy form.

What color is the energy?

Yellows and yellow-purple.

Are their any physical objects in the room?

There's a desk. I'm sitting at a desk and he's standing. No he's sitting now, or at least he's lower.

Is he going to review your past-life?

Yes, that's what we are doing.

At what point in the past-life are you starting?

Starting at the death. It's telepathic, as though we see it together.

What happens next?

We are stopping at various points.

What's discussed?

It's when I left my parents. They died and I left and ran away. He said I didn't need to have run away. It would have been OK to stay.

Is this something you understand or do you need more information?

I understand. I understand I was very young and ran away because I didn't have anyone. I think my guide's pleased with the rest of my life. He liked the way I talked. He said I talked with love and that was good for me.

What was the learning about this running away?

[Pause] My parents died in an accident but it was not my fault. I ran away because I did not want others to think it was my fault. He knows that. I dedicated my life then to helping other people.

Ask your guide what was planned to happen when your parents died?

It was so that I would learn to stand on my own feet. So I could learn independence.

So it did not matter if you stayed or not?
*No. I still learnt the lesson. I had a good life and I learnt a
lot and was independent, but I still needed that family.*
Does anything else happen with your guide?
I just feel good when I'm with him.

Clients of spiritual regression report that the soul is immortal and
has a vibrating swirling energy that can be perceived with
different colors. Grayish for younger souls through a range of
colors including yellow, orange and greens to purple for the more
experienced ones. Souls can also show themselves in a human or
semi human shape by projecting their thoughts into the energy. In
a similar way the setting can be in its normal energy form or
perceived in a human form that provides comfort, such as a garden
or temple. In Heather's review with her spirit guide it was sitting
at a table.

All spiritual regressions will be different from each other to
some extent. Exploring them has similarities to exploring a past-
life, and it's normally best to allow the soul memories to emerge
in the order they were experienced from the death in one life to the
birth in the next life:

What happens next?

**Let me know if there are any other significant events
happening here before we move on?**

Whilst various suggestions for questions are offered in this book,
many questions will follow naturally from what the client says.
Careful listening is needed. So if the client talks about seeing
energy say, 'Describe this energy' or 'Do you recognize this
energy' rather than 'Who are these helpers'. Questions are best
kept to open ended ones and need to be clearly stated. The

remarkable thing about soul memories is that they often have a high level of visual content. An example that illustrates this is a client who is color blind in their current-life and unable to distinguish purple from blue, and brown from red. In his soul memories he was amazed to discover he could see and distinguish all the separate colors from each other. Often clients will experience far more than they talk about, so it is best to allow plenty of time for the response to a question.

Heather was met by her spirit guide and taken to a holding space with lots of other souls until the review of her past-life took place. Sometimes souls go straight to the review, while the more experienced souls may skip this part and immediately go to a library and review the past-life in a book. Often this will be a solitary activity with the further review happening at a later time. Even with Heather's past-life that seemed peaceful and complete, the review still took place because it forms the basis of many of the soul activities before the next incarnation.

Clients who have not communicated with their spirit guide before will find the experience will stay with them for the rest of their lives:

Do you have any thoughts of who has met you?

As Heather found, it was a profound experience beyond words. Sometimes called teachers, they have a very close relationship with the soul. They know what is planned for the life and often provide intuitive help and guidance during the physical incarnation. Sometimes they show themselves in human form to make the incoming soul more comfortable:

Is your guide showing itself in physical or energy form?

Describe the facial features or energy in detail.

114

Spiritual names tend to be permanent and have a special meaning. Oscar's guide was called Zenestra, a name he initially found difficult to pronounce. This is not uncommon so encouragement is needed.

Frequently the past-life review is done with the spirit guide. The communication is telepathic although some souls report it's like watching a film or video. In some cases souls say it was like stepping into the life again, which allows them to remember the emotions in more detail. As the past-life is reviewed its an opportunity to bring karmic learning to the client's conscious awareness:

Does your guide review your past-life with you?

Did you achieve its purpose?

What problems did you have?

During a profound spiritual encounter with their spirit guide the client may stop talking and be engulfed in the experience. In order to ensure that information is recorded they need to be encouraged to report back on what is happening.

Sometimes the client's personality will try to answer the questions and they may report seeing a religious icon such as 'Christ' or an 'Angel'. This is more likely to happen if the level of trance has not been deep enough. Spirits of light can show themselves in may forms but clients may be quick to interpret the spiritual experience based on their own religious beliefs. It is important to respect a person's inner world so I simply encouraged them to stay with the experience for a short time and describe what they experience, rather than form quick judgments.

If its necessary to deepen the trance at this point the therapist can have an 'eternal now' discussion directly with the spirit guide via the client:

I'm going to ask your guide to communicate directly with me.

As the client channels information from the spirit guide it disassociates their conscious mind. In addition it is possible to ask for the client's immortal spirit name and then some of the questions can be directed to the spirit name. This further dissociates the client's conscious mind and deepens the experience.

MEETING SOUL GROUPS

After the past life review Heather's spiritual regression continues with meeting her soul group. These are souls who she has worked with over many incarnations, some of whom she recognizes in this life. Their human names have been changed:

Where do you go next?
I'm with lots of my group.
My group?
My mum's there. It's good to see her again.
Are they showing themselves in human form?
No. I just know who they are.
Describe the colors?
They are sort of pale yellow, but some pinky-yellow.
How many are there?
I think there's about 20, but others are nearby.
Just stay with the group you are with. Who do you recognize?

Greg. [son from this life] *They are making themselves more human. John's there* [friend]. *Dad. Grant* [ex husband]. *My parents. My parents-in-law. Bob* [early boyfriend] *and Stuart.* [her other son]

What about Janet? Lesa? Carla? [from the list of characters supplied in the interview]

Yes. It's good to see Carla.

What are your energy colors?

A pinky color.

Is it similar or different in any way to your group?

Similar.

How many lifetimes have you been together with this group?

A long time, I want to say 46.

What's the common learning theme?

Peace.

Was the past-life you just experienced something to do with peace?

Yes, because the independence brought me great peace. I was peaceful.

Do you recognize any of your soul group working out in the past-life?

Bob was Charles. My mum was Mary.

Is there anything else that happens of significance with your soul group before you leave them?

No.

Are there any other soul groups you work with?

There are. They are all yellow, slightly different colors from our group.

Go there. Who do you recognize from that group?

Ian. [husband] *Ruby.* [ex husband's new wife]

What is the purpose of this soul group?

They seem to be the challenges.

Find Ruby. What do you say to her?

[smiled] *She did a good job.*

Is it just this life you have worked with her?

She's been there quite a bit.

What challenges has she given you in this life?

She reminds me?

What does she remind you?

She works to balance me in some way.

What's it like to meet her in soul form?

It's my antagonism. It's almost as if we laugh at each other. She's good at what she does.

Check out if this is something you asked her to do?

Yes. When I left Grant I took his children away from him and she took my children Stuart and Greg away from me. She works with Greg quite a lot. [surprised voice] *It was Greg who came up with this idea.*

When the regression leads to a meeting with the soul group, the client will often report approaching a group of lights. This is a profound experience and many clients talk about being 'back home'.

Souls have different soul energy colors, which are not solid and often described as swirling and moving. If clients are asked to look closely at the core they are able to pick out the colors more clearly. Sometimes it may even be necessary to ask for the movement to be slowed so that the different colors can be identified. This is useful because the colors represent the experiences and development of the soul. Knowledge of these colors helps to identify the type of soul group the client has met. Souls with similar colors belong to a *primary soul group.* Generally these souls will have been working with this type of group for many life times and the reunions are spiritually intense. Some variation in color may be noted because not all the souls in a group progress at an equal rate. Those that advance faster spend less and less time with their primary soul group and more time with other soul groups. When they appear along with the original soul group they may appear darker or their colors may take on different hues:

Focus on them one by one and describe the colors?

Is this the same as yours?

What do you experience as you join them?

Sometimes souls come together from different groups to work cooperatively on particular karmic aspects. The way to spot these groups is that the members will have different soul energy colors. In Heather's case she called this her challenge group. It is useful to use the client's list of characters, particularly those that they have had negative experiences with in this life, because many of these souls will be recognized in these encounters. Heather recognized Ruby with whom she had repeated conflicts in this life. She gained new insights when she recalled that it was the soul of her son Greg who had come up with the idea that had caused her so much conflict in this life. Importantly it had been with her agreement at a soul level. Discovering that key events in this life are pre planned has enormous implications to the conscious mind:

Focus on your soul group one by one and tell me the names of any that you recognize in your current-life.

VISIT TO THE ELDERS

Returning to Oscar's spiritual regression of the blacksmith executed by the Romans. It is picked up at the point he meets the elders with his spirit guide Zenestra:

Go to the point when you meet the spirits of light who planned your current-life incarnation.
I'm in the front of a table that's in an arch shape.
Look around the room and tell me if it's in energy or physical form?
It's just a room, a white room.
Look upwards and tell me what you see?
Purple shimming energy. Like waves.
Do you get a sense of what this energy is?
It's all powerful, all knowing. I'm but a drop in its ocean.
Are you able to connect with this energy or are others connecting with this energy?
[Pause] *Others I think. I am connected with it but not in thought.*
Who else is in this room with you?
Zenestra.
Is she by your side or behind you?
Floats between, behind and by my side.
Look in front of you and tell me how many spirits of light that there are?
Six.
How are they showing themselves, in energy or human form?
Human form.
Describe them and start with the one that is most prominent?

A black man, with big blob of black hair on top of him. The next is an elderly lady with fair hair and light blue eyes. Another lady with a sort of a teacher's smile, a benevolent smile. Her hair is done up in a bun. Then there's an elderly man and he is bold.

And the others?

Middle Eastern looking with big bushy eyebrows and short black hair, and an elderly looking lady at the end with a sort of black veil over her head. Her face has lots of lines in it.

Which one of these will be communicating to you?

The one who looks like a teacher.

Look very closely and see if there are any ornaments or anything decorative?

She's wearing something in her hair. It's what women put in their hair when they have a bun.

A pin?

Yes it's like a big pin, a golden pin.

What's the significance of the golden pin?

It's like a treble clef, that's a musical key.

What does it mean to you?

My passion for life is music. It always has been. It's my most intimate companion in life, and either complements my moods or adjusts them.

What's the dialogue you have?

Spirit are asking me why am I afraid.

Are they referring to this life or other lives?

This life.

What's your answer to that?

I'll not achieve.

What's their answer?

What do you want to achieve?

What do you say to them?

To leave something behind that will benefit people for a long time and remember me.

What do they say in reply?

Haven't you done so already?

Ask them to review this live and amplify that point. Tell me what they say?

You were given love, warmth and protection from your mother who needed to give it. You gave everyone that love, warmth and protection. Your happiness lay in giving other people happiness, and by giving other people happiness that prevailed over what you wanted to be or who you where. You started to see yourself and do things through other people's eyes even though it was not expected of you. So you embarked on this path, this career doing it at the expense of your identity and needs. You have now reached the point of separation between making others happy, but for a change making yourself happy too. You now need to bridge the gap between the two. It can be bridged, and you will bridge it. So be brave and continue to learn.

Do you understand now?

I understand

Can the fear go?

Yes.

The most important part of a soul's experience between lives is meeting the spirits of light who have a level of experience and wisdom that not does require them to physically reincarnate. They review the progress of the soul before them and can replay any of its past lives and discus aspects until the soul understands what will be expected for the next life. Usually the client will have this meeting at least once between lives. Some of the names they are called include 'elders', 'higher ones', 'masters' or the 'wise ones'. Sometimes the client will not have a name for them but just report having to go to an important meeting. Writers have called them the 'council of elders'[3] or the 'karmic committee'[4]. If the client uses a particular name then this can be used. If a name is not offered I find the safest way to refer to them in a spiritual regression as, 'the spirits of light that plan the next reincarnation'. In the following text the name 'elders' will be used to collectively refer to them.

Often the client will report their spirit guide has joined them and they are moving off together which can be an indicator of going to meet the elders. This meeting can occur at any point in the spiritual regression, but often happens after the reunion with the soul groups. A client can be asked to skip to this point at any time. This was particularly useful with Oscar's regression because it was used to leave his soul memories following the Roman past-life and to move to his soul memories prior to incarnating in this life:

Go to the place where you meet the wise spirits of light who planned your current-life incarnation.

It is useful to ask many questions about the location and description of the spirits of light that are met. This sets the scene before starting the dialogue and increases the 'reality' of the experience when the client is replaying tapes of the session later:

Describe your travel route. Let me know what you see and what happens when you arrive?

Describe the surroundings you find yourself in?

The number and appearance of the elders is important. Often they project an appearance or wear a brooch or ornament that has a symbolic meaning for the client. This can be very profound. One client even arranged to have a brooch handmade in the style of the one she had seen to remind her of the message.

Time needs to be spent in asking detailed questions. In Oscar's meeting, one of the elders was wearing a golden pin in the shape of a treble cleft to remind him of the importance of music in balancing his emotions. Possible questions include:

Look closely. Are they in energy form or physical form?

Describe the faces of each one.

Describe how they are dressed and any ornament or emblem you notice.

What is the significance of that ornament or emblem to you?

What is communicated to you in this meeting?

This type of review is broader than the initial review by the spirit guide after crossing over and sets the basis for the next life that the client will have. Sometimes whole strings of previous lives may be reviewed for a soul to understand what will be expected of them.

In Oscar's meeting with the elders the questions were switched to what he was afraid of in his current-life. This is referred to as working in the 'eternal now' and will be covered later. Nothing can be hidden and the soul knows this absolutely. Notice the compassionate way they offered advice to Oscar and the love that came from that meeting which was overpowering.

BODY SELECTION FOR THE CURRENT-LIFE

Returning to Heather's spiritual regression. It is taken up at the point when preparations are being made for her current-life:

Go to the place where you selected your body for this life. Then describe the place you find yourself.
It's like there are some screens and dials. Big screens. My guide is there with me.
How many bodies do you have to choose from?
Three.
Tell me about the other two bodies other than the one you are in now?
One is a tall man.
What sort of life will that be?
Oh no. I don't want that one.
What was wrong with that body?
I didn't like being so tall. I would be stooping down all the time, but it would be a gentle body.
What about the second one?
I seem very ordinary.
Is it a man or woman?
A woman. Very plain and a bit simple actually. I don't understand why that was an option. No, I don't want that life.
What were the family circumstances of that life?
It was a quite united family.
Would it have given you a strong base to start from?
Yes. A lot of love in that family. A simple non-materialistic life.
Was the body you are in now the third one?
Yes.

125

Why did you pick that one?

Because my parents would be who they are and they would be in lives that would really complement my plan, because my father would be a teacher and my mother a nurse. I know that they would give me a happy childhood with a very strong platform.

Did you have any choice of intelligence or emotions?

I did not need too much intelligence.

Was that your choice?

Yes.

What would have happened if you had lots of intelligence?

I would have been distracted and become materialistic.

What about emotions?

I chose to be very level and balanced.

Was that your choice or your guide's choice?

It was mine.

Does your guide agree with your choice?

Yes.

And in picking the body for this life was their any knowledge of weight being a problem? [Being overweight had been discussed in the interview]

Yes.

So you knew about this problem before you reincarnated?

Yes, because the parents I choose have weight problems. With all the other things being right that was less of a concern.

This is the place where the soul can try out the body for the next life and sometimes have a choice in its selection. Some clients describe seeing bodies in front of them, or like watching a video or screen. However they describe it, this telepathic experience gives them a greater understanding about themselves and their origin. At some point during the spiritual regression the soul leaves to visit this place. Often it's during the meeting with the elders, or the client can be asked to go straight there:

Go to the place where you select your body for this life.

The level of choice by the soul in this process depends on their experience. Understanding why their body and family in this life was selected is particularly important for clients with physical problems or those with family difficulties:

How many body choices do you have?

What do you think each body offers you?

Do you have a choice of the life or family or circumstances with each body?

If you have a choice of bodies why do you pick one and reject the others?

DEPARTING FOR REINCARNATION

This is a short extract from a client I'll call Anne. She was a 30-year-old woman from Denmark who had specifically asked for the spiritual regression to include how she reincarnated. It taken up at the point of her current-life planning:

Where do you go next?
I must now go and plan my next life. My guide is taking me to a cinema where I can see and choose.
Is this your current-life you are planning for?
Yes it is. We have discussed that I must work with the same issue. It's so I know what the life will be about.

Remind me what the issue is.

I must be able to let my soul come through in a balanced way.

How does the process of planning work?

I think I can choose between two lives.

Look at the first body. Tell about it.

It's a girl.

What sort of body is it?

Just a normal body.

What sort of life will it be?

The girl will be on her own. Not many from my soul group will attend, but I will be well educated.

In what way will you be well educated?

I will go to law school and have a career, and at some point allow the soul to come through.

What do you reject about that life?

It's a very controlled life and very mental. It's difficult to feel emotions.

What will that mean?

It will be very difficult for the soul to go through that mental brain. There will not be much support around because they will all be intellectual.

Will it be a hard life?

Yes. I'm not sure I can get through with my soul energy.

Do you have to take a lot of soul energy?

Yes

Did you discuss how much?

At least 70 per cent.

Have you ever taken that level of soul energy down before?

No.

What will be the risk of taking so much soul energy down?

I cannot continue my work at home in the spirit world.

So you can do work in the spirit world at the same time as being reincarnated?

Yes.

Move onto the other body. The one you have for this life. What was your first impression of it?

Some weakness.

What was the weakness?

It was a soft personality that will go in the direction of the wind.

Any other impressions?

It was still a nice body, normal size and normal intelligence.

Did the family circumstances come with this or did you have to work that out yourself?

I knew there would be several soul group members with me.

What would be the benefit of having several group members with this body?

We can help each other.

Did you discuss with your guide how much energy would need to be brought down with this body?

Yes. I could use 35 per cent.

Does that present any risks for you?

Yes. I may not be able to maintain the purpose I came for. That was why it was important to have group members to help.

Which body offered you most spiritual growth?

The one I'm in. The country of Denmark that goes with this body is more open minded and there was no danger from nature or wars. It is a protected life so I can focus on the purpose.

[At this point I'm skipping to a later part of the spiritual regression]

I'd like you to move to the point when you are doing your preparations for starting your current-life. Are you by yourself or with your spirit guide?

I say good-bye to my spirit guide [sighs] *and I go on my own.*

Where do you go?

To a room where there are all sort of colors. It's so relaxed and in harmony. I think I get a healing once more.

This healing. In what way is it going to help you in what is going to happen?

It's because it will be a difficult birth and I need some extra help to enter the little body.

Are you taking some extra energy with you?

Yes. It will also help the mother to cope with it.

When do you know that the time is ready to go and join the little body?

I will get a sign from the others.

Are some energy forms in this room with you?

Yes. They know when it is time to go. When the baby is ready.

Go to that time and tell me what happens?

I go into a tunnel of light and I move through that tunnel. I am so far away and can feel the body of the little child and I will try and enter.

What part do you enter first?

The head. Trying to come into the head.

Do you know how many months from conception this child is?

I think it's six months' old?

As you enter what starts to happen?

We try and merge with each other. It's a very soft meeting.

How does this compare with other babies you have merged with before?

This is going very easy, the baby is very cooperative.
Do you normally join at six months or do you sometimes join earlier or later?
I think I sometimes join earlier.
What's the earliest you have joined before?
Three months. I had to do much preparation to go into the baby.
Are their any problems of joining before three months?
Yes. Its not so developed the baby. It's not so finished and something can still happen.
What's the oldest it's ever been?
Seven months.
What happens after seven months?
It's hard to join. You must force it more.
Are there problems of forcing it more?
It's not the way I like to do it. I like to be gentle.
Does it cause any physical problems with the baby if you have to force it more?
It could, but I won't take any risks that are not planned.

All humans have their own unique soul that can split in two parts. Some of the soul energy is taken into the next reincarnation, and the other part remains in the spirit realms. The amount that is taken into reincarnation will affect the type of life. The less energy that is taken the less influence the soul can have on the physical life and harder it will be to achieve the karmic purpose for that life. The soul energy remaining in the spirit realms can carry out spiritual activities such as continuing to learn for future lives or working with soul groups. The level of this activity will depend upon the percentage left, and the higher it is the greater the activity. Thus a multi-dimensional reality occurs with the soul operating in both the spirit realms and in human incarnation:

Tell me where you go while you wait to leave the spirit realms to reincarnate into your current-life.

What percentage of your soul energy will you be taking with you?

What is the reason for taking that level of energy into this reincarnation?

The split is not absolute because the soul maintains an energetic link between the parts called intuition, and like a hologram retain its wholeness. The level of energy to take into the new life may be planned between the spirit guide and the soul, but is often reviewed or set by the elders because they have accesses to information on the wider implications of the planned life. After death in a life, the soul energies may reunify during the period of energy rejuvenation or at a later point. Sometimes it may be described as a shower of energy or just an expansion and feeling whole again.

The joining of soul energy with a physical body usually takes place when the body is in its most malleable stage, around four months after conception. Attached to the soul energy will be any unresolved subtle body memories from past lives. The percentage of unresolved past-life memories that will be imprinted onto the baby is part of the planning process for the new life. The greater the percentage the more difficult the life will be. The fusion with the baby's biological inherited characteristics produces the foundation of the personality for the new life:

What emotions or physical memories will you be taking from your past lives?

What percentage of these will you be taking with you?

What is the reason for taking that level into this reincarnation?

At the time of fusion between the soul energy and the baby's body an amnesiac memory block is put in place by the soul. This stops the person from being overwhelmed from all the traumatic past lives that they are not ready to assimilate at a conscious level[3]. It also allows the new life to be an opportunity to find new solutions to old karmic problems. The memory block can be a gradual process that becomes complete during early childhood:

Go to the point when your soul energy merges with the physical baby in the womb and tell me about the experience.

How will you remember the significant people you need to meet in this life?

Discovering that at a soul level a client was involved with choosing the physical body, life circumstances and the difficulty of the life gives them new insights. One client reported:

'I had a definite sense of moving to a different space than I've had with past-life experiences, and embracing different layers. The insight and understanding that was available to me is beyond words. It was like being given a hint of something far greater, and as this realization sank in the effect on me was immense'.

OTHER SPIRITUAL ACTIVITIES

With more reincarnation experiences, souls increasingly move away from the focus of working with their soul groups. They may start to train in various areas of specialization[5] in the spirit realms, and be more involved in the planning process for the next life. One client recalled being in a soul group doing research into the soul and physical body merger, and experimented over a number of past lives with different levels of energy using various types of bodies. Another client recalled going to another planetary system to be taught about working with energy. Sometimes souls go to a place of solitude for study and reflection, or they may be involved in teaching other souls or going to halls of learning.

A Hybrid Soul is the name given to a special class of soul by Michael Newton[6]. These are old souls whose former planets have been destroyed or they may have come to Earth because of the special physical and mental challenges of the complexity of the human condition in the modern world. As soul energy, they can merge with the baby like other souls, although some may have trouble adapting which can lead to severe psychological problems. Many adapt and lead productive lives and report that their last life was on another planet, not necessarily in a physical form. Needless to say the process of review with the elders, soul groups and body selection may not follow the patterns indicated in the previous part of the chapter. I am deliberately not including more information in the book about them because they rarely occur and when they do, I have found that the best approach is to take the role of an inquisitive investigator and allow the story to emerge without any preconceptions of what will happen.

WORKING IN THE 'ETERNAL NOW'

The therapist can direct the regression to the meeting with the elders at any time and enter into an interactive dialogue called the 'eternal now'. This enables specific questions to be asked for the benefit of the client. It can be left until after the soul memories have been explored to make it clearer when the client listens to the recording afterwards:

> **Go to the meeting with the elders.** (or the name given by the client)

With the intuitive link flowing strongly in the altered state of awareness from hypnosis and the spiritual regression it is an opportunity to ensure that the client has all the information they need from the session:

> **Ask them to confirm what your purpose is for your current-life.**
>
> **What comments do they have about your progress in this life?**
>
> **Do they offer any more advise to help you in this life?**

Questions about the client's spiritual future can also be asked. However, at some point the flow of information may suddenly stop when the elders consider it will interfere with the clients freewill or when they have enough information to work with:

> **Can they tell you about your spiritual activities in the future?**

If one of the client's objectives is to improve communication with their spirit guide this can be done in the eternal now. The therapist can direct the regression to the meeting with the spirit guide and guide the basic communication. This can form the foundation for the client's later work in meditation:

Ask your spirit guide for advice on how to improve your communication with it.

Before finishing a spiritual regression it is worth checking with the client that everything has been covered:

Before we leave the spirit realms I want you to tell me if there is any last question you want to ask any of the spirits of light?

A COMPLETE SPIRITUAL REGRESSION

A client I'll call Clare was a 32-year-old solicitor. She had made a major life change six months earlier and was now training to be a complementary therapist. She had experienced several past-life regressions and now wanted to know about her karmic progress and if she was on the right track spiritually. She had brought a list of eight significant people in her life that included her husband, family members, previous boyfriends and mother-in-law. Below is a major part of the transcript of her session.

Going quickly into deep trance she regressed into a past-life of a mercenary soldier working in Russia. The soldier was escorting some important Russian nobility and Mongols had ambushed the party. In the ensuing fight he was killed:

It's a beautiful light.
Does the light come to you or do you go to the light?

We move towards each other.

And what happens as you move to each other?

Although there's no human form, I feel the shape has arms to embrace me. It's as if it's expanding. I'm just drawn to go to the sensation of love.

Is it a gentle or strong pull?

I feel I'm being drawn by my heart and feel a hand is guiding me from behind.

And are you aware of anything else?

Moving away from the earth, a beautiful light moving away from the earth. I'm so far away now. Just colors.

What colors are you aware of with this energy form that has met you?

Hints of colors, blues, purples and greens.

Do you have an awareness of who this energy is?

It's ... it's my teacher.

And is it your teacher who has been overseeing you in that past-life?

He's been sending me messages. Hints.

What does he communicate to you?

He seems quite happy. It seems like it's gone quite well.

Check out what you were meant to learn in that life, and have a review with him.

Its about duty, honor, respect and teamwork.

What are you aware of as you have this review?

Sitting around a table. He looks different now.

What does he look like?

He's quite young, a little older than me. He's strong, male.

Does he show himself in any particular clothing?

He's wearing lumberjack clothing, quite casual.

Why is he showing himself in this form?

It's a form I'm comfortable with. I can speak more easily like this. It's not so overwhelming as when he showed himself as energy.

How does he review the past-life with you?

Part telepathically and part spoken. Anything that's important for us to review we speak about, but anything else he communicates telepathically to me. He just lets me know its OK.

At what part of the past-life does he start from?

He's doing this backward with me starting at the death.

How well do you think you did in that life, now that you have reviewed it with your guide?

I'm quite happy. I made a couple of wrong decisions on the way but I came to the right conclusion. I'm not very happy about having killed.

Tell me what happens in the discussion with your guide about having killed?

He says its part of the life I chose. He's asking how I expected to be in an army and not kill.

What do you say about that?

In that life I thought I was doing it for honorable reasons, but now I feel sad.

Ask your guide what he says about you feeling sad?

He says its OK, it shows compassion and he tells me that I should know that everyone makes their choices. He's showing me that the men who attacked us in the final battle felt that it was a great honor to be doing what they were doing. They chose to fight in the same way that I chose to fight. We all knew the risks.

Do you understand now?

It's difficult when I've just left a human form. There's just a small hint of the physical still with me. My guide says its

OK and will fade. I haven't finished what he calls 'the debrief and integration' yet.

Move onto to the next part and tell me what happens.

There are others.

Describe where you are and the others with you?

It's difficult to describe. It's like a big dome. It's just made of energy. It's everywhere.

What other aspects are you aware of other than the dome?

There are lots of people.

What are they doing?

Floating. It's not like a solid floor its just waves.

Are the others showing themselves in human form or energy form?

Energy form.

Are you comfortable with them being in that form?

Yes.

Describe what these energy forms are like.

Vibrant, radiant, translucent.

Are there any particular colors coming from them?

They seem to be different colors. As they communicate the colors change.

How many are there in this dome? Count them.

[Long pause] *Sixty-seven.*

What position are they in relative to you?

It's like three clusters. Some are in a semicircle on my left, some to the back of me and to the right, and there's another cluster just floating a little higher.

What are you doing in this place?

I want to see my friends and they all seemed to have known I was coming.

What do you experience?

It feels like a huge hug. I'm so happy to be back with them.

How many members of this cluster are there?

Twenty-six in all.

Is their something you are all trying to learn together in this soul group?

It's about helping.

How many lifetimes have you been with them?

Fifty-three.

Look at some of the colors in this group and describe them?

Translucent silver, the same as my energy.

Do you recognize any of this group in your last past-life?

Yes, two were my friends in the army. A lot of them reincarnated at the same time but in different places.

Where any of them in the army that you were fighting?

Yes. There were five of them. [laughs lightly] They think it was funny because we called them Barbarians. They called us Barbarians too.

What are your thoughts now about your army friends here and those who fought against you?

It was about being true to our causes. Although it was difficult in the groups we were in, we were trying to spread friendship and compassion, and lots of little deeds of love and help to friends and family.

Is there anything else you need to know about those companions?

No.

How many of your soul group are in reincarnation in this life now?

Seven.

Do you recognize them?

Yes. We will be working together.

Ask them what the work will be?

Trying to spread love and light to as many people as possible, by trying to touch them in some way. It's hard to describe. To be open to every opportunity to open to understanding, healing for our self and others.

Is their anything else you need to know from this group?

No. It's good just to be with them.

Move to the point when you join the other soul group. What are you doing with them?

This is a lively group. We all challenge each other.

How many of you are there in this soul group?

Twenty-one.

And look at the colors of this group. Have they all the same colors or different energy colors?

Different colors.

What is the purpose of this group?

This is my learning group.

Is there a specific aspect that this group are learning now?

There have been a few. We are all working on tolerance at the moment.

What aspects have you worked on before?

Truth, love, regret, happiness. These are the main ones.

Do you recognize any of this group working out in your current-life?

I recognize eight energies but I can only place four of them.

Lets work with the four you can place. Select one and tell me what you say to them, and what they say to you.

We are just laughing at the problems we had in the past. It's so unimportant now.

Was this something that had been planned?

Yes.

Bring the others forward one by one and discuss with them about the problems in this lifetime.

It's a very difficult discussion. They cannot speak to me.

Are they able to bring any of the memories when you planned to work together?

We gathered with our teachers and all said what we needed to learn. If there was a match and two could work together that was easy. If more of us were needed we talked about it. Sometimes there was not a match in our group and then one might volunteer into a role to help.

Did you need to know what body you would be having before you agreed to work together?

You get an idea of the form you need. An easy example is if you are going to be an abuser and you need to use force you have a strong body. If you are going to be a victim you would have a weaker body.

Go to that place where you choose a body for this life and tell me what you see and what happens?

It's a room made of energy. In part of the room you can look at images.

How do you know what bodies you can pick?

Just like a generic form and then you have different option such as short, fat, thin. Once you have sorted that out you can go into the detail.

How many specific options do you have offered to you in this life?

Three. I could have been a man, quite frail, in a non-loving family. I could have been a girl, quite large with an abusive family. The body and family that I have now was the third choice.

What made you pick the body and family you have right now?

I wanted a strong base for this life. I felt that this would give me the support to overcome the difficult parts.

Are the difficult parts to do with tolerance?

Some are about tolerance for me, and some about tolerance towards others.

Would you have been able to work with tolerance with the other bodies?

I thought I might have failed in the other bodies.

Did you have any choice about the type of brain or emotions you would have?

Yes.

How did you go about selecting those?

I didn't have a choice over intelligence. My teacher decided that. For emotions I had two choices. Either full access to feel everything about myself and other peoples situations or to be quite hard.

Who's choice was it in the end?

My teacher and I agreed. It would have been easy to be hard. I wanted to experience all the emotions and my teacher agreed?

Are their any other decisions, parents for example?

The type of parents went with the body that was chosen. The actual parents were chosen for me.

Did you have any trial run before making the final decision?

Yes I had to. I don't know how to describe it. I experienced the feelings. It was like in a form of meditation. Some of them were not so nice.

Do you understand why you had the body, mind, emotions and parents you have in this life?

Yes.

Once you had made that decision did you have to go back to your soul group and let them know about it?

They all seemed to know somehow.

Did you do any role-play in the bodies with your soul group?

Not this time. I have in other lives.

What was the purpose of role-play before coming into reincarnation?

So that the energy gets imprinted of what you really need to do. When you incarnate you don't remember. It's like imprinting the driving force that kicks in when you have to make decisions. It kicks out a feeling you should go one way and not another.

Is their anything else you need to say to the soul group on tolerance before we leave them?

Goodbye. See you soon.

Move to the point of joining the third of the groups and tell me what do you do in that group?

I feel very humble in this group. This group are the overseers of the other two groups.

Are they different from your teacher?

No. My teacher is part of them.

Are any in reincarnation at the moment?

Only one that I can place.

Will you have any work with this one?

Yes.

Do you recognize who it is?

Yes. [surprised voice] *It's the baby that I'm carrying.*

Is there anything you need to find out, any questions you have for them? Tell me a summary of those discussions.

It's already unfolding. I'm trying to ask if I actively need to do anything to bring it about.

If your teacher is permitted to tell you, ask what you will be doing in the near future.

They cannot tell me exactly. I've just got to watch out for the opportunities. I will just feel it when they are presented.

Thank them all for their information and help. Go to the place where the spirits of light are who planned your incarnation in this life, and describe the place.

It's another dome.

How many energy shapes are there?

Seven.

Do they show themselves in human form or spiritual form?

They are in energy form.

Describe what you are aware of around these energy forms?

The magnitude of their energy is distracting me. The dome does not look all that different than the other one, but it feels very different.

Focus on that energy in the dome and describe this energy.

It's from the source. It's too strong for me to get closer. It's just overwhelming. It connects right in with your heart.

Other than the dome what else are you aware of around these energy forms?

The floor in its physical from is like marble. In other times there would be a table, but it's not here now. Also big tall-backed chairs.

What colors are these energies?

Just pure brilliant light.

Is your teacher with you?

Yes.

Tell what happens in this encounter?

My teacher is like my advocate.

What does he say?

He reminds them of the work that we are all doing, particularly the work I have been doing.

What particular things does you teacher say about your work?

He said I did ... it's difficult to hear ... I did well to help my other energy friend in his quest. He says as much as my actions amuse him I need to continue working on tolerance.

In how many past lives have you been working on tolerance?

At some level for three.

Can you ask the wise spirits of light to recap these lives so that you understand what happened in each?

I'm getting an influx of information. I've seen tolerance from what you could describe as violent angles. The first life I was not tolerated. I just could not get people to see me for what I was. They could not see beyond how I looked. I learned that I could not expect people to change their views and opinions because I told them. I also learned that it did not matter what people thought of me. In the next life I choose to play the other role, and be intolerant, so I could experience the opposite.

What sort of person were you in that life?

I was horrible. I was a woman who just would not accept anyone who was different in color, shape and disability. I even looked down on people who had not made much of their lives or anyone who lived in any way different to the way I lived.

What was the third one?

This life.

Can you ask the spirits of light what they say about your last two lives and this life?

I've done most of the work. It's the smaller scales that I need to keep aware of.

What smaller things are they referring to?

Mostly I've thought of tolerances as big things such as people's different color or culture. I'm now learning that I need to be tolerant of every ones views and opinions. I'm now trying to understand why someone has those views rather than think they are rude. That some thing may have happened if someone has a lot to say or little to say.

Do the spirits of light have any advise to help you?

To keep my awareness around me. To recognize the situations and learn from them.

Do you understand that?

Yes I do.

Do they have anything else to say to you?

They seem quite satisfied.

Is their anything else you need to ask the spirits of light?

I need more confidence.

Ask them if they will show you a past-life that will help?

They are showing a past-life when I was strong. I felt like I could do anything.

Are you feeling this strength now?

I'm feeling it in my chest now.

Remember this feeling and past-life whenever you need to be reminded of your strength.

They are nodding with recognition. Telepathically they are giving me the feeling that they are satisfied and for me just to keep going.

Are any of them able to tell you in detail the spiritual things you will be doing in the near future?

They are really happy about the ones I'm involved with, and the training and development work that I'm doing in this life. I'm being told I need to get about more, have more confidence in my abilities. Not to worry about getting things wrong. If the intensions are right it doesn't matter.

Do they give you any specific information?

I'll have an opportunity to meet someone I thought I would never meet.

Are they permitted to tell you more?

Something to do with psychic development.

In what way will this person help?

Inspiration and just by being in the energy of this person their will be an attunement and raising of my vibrations.

Is this enough information?

Yes. I think they have probably told me more than they should.

Is there any last question you have for the spirits of light?

No.

Let's thank them for their wisdom and insight and release them from this meeting.

Clare did go on to have her baby, meet a psychic teacher as predicted and is busy doing spiritual work with some of her soul group members. This is what Clare wrote about her spiritual regression afterwards:

Although I feel that my words cannot do it justice, if I had to find a way to express my feelings on paper it would be that the spiritual regression was an extremely profound experience. It put a lot of what I perceived as 'issues' in my life into context and enabled me to have a look at the bigger picture of my life.

I had the amazing opportunity to glimpse into my life between lives, to see the process of making choices and the procedures that are in place to ensure that we make the most of our incarnate time on earth. I had a glimpse of my soul groups, to stand face to face with my karma group in a place of love and understanding and non-judgment, to meet my council of elders and open up channels of communication with my guide. It was just magical and wondrous and it has left me with such a deep respect for the strength of the universe and for the process that is in play each time we make a choice to come back to earth. It has given me a renewed respect for myself and the choices that I have made and a deeper love for my friends, family and my challengers in this life, my sisters and brothers on this journey.

Most magically for me, I feel that this work was able to touch not only myself, but also my baby who I was carrying at the time of the spiritual regression session. We already have an understanding of each other even before she has been born. Everything will be perfect and is in place for her part of this journey. I do not spend my time worrying about physical or practical aspects of pregnancy and am not frightened about childbirth. We have seen each other's souls and are ready to work together. I cannot describe how free I feel to enjoy every moment of this pregnancy.

As I write this I realize that this work has touched me on an even deeper level than I had realized. I feel re-connected, I know where I am, I know why I came, I know that the choices I make are perfect at the time I make them and I know that I am loved.

SUMMARY

A spiritual regression is not focused at resolving a complex. This is the therapeutic aim of regression therapy. However, it gives the client a profound insight of their souls evolution and purpose for this life. It also goes further and gives them an opportunity to review their progress in this life and receive spiritual guidance from the elders. Through this greater understanding and seeing the wider picture comes the opportunity for them to change their current-life and consequently start the process of soul healing and resolving their complexes. Although some clients may spontaneously remember some soul memories during a past-life regression, for most the intuitive link needs to be enhanced by using deep hypnosis to get the depth of detail. However, the intuitive link established in a past-life regression allows for an interactive dialogue with the spirit guide. This opens the way for

149

aspects of a spiritual regression to be integrated into regression therapy.

Many of the key questions to navigate the soul memories are shown in Appendix III. Through experience and intuition many questions will naturally follow the clients responses. The simplest way to navigate is by asking, 'What happens next' and 'Let me know if any other significant events happen here before we move on'. Listening to what the client says is important so it can be used in the reply. If the client says, 'I can see energy' saying 'Do you recognize this energy' or 'Describe this energy' is preferable to leading questions like, 'Who is this helper'. Clients in deep hypnosis may be slow in responding to questions so they need to be given time to respond fully before the next question is asked. To speed up the spiritual regression guiding questions can be asked to take the client directly to key events such as the meeting with the spirit guide, soul groups, the elders and the place of body selection. Normally its best to allow the soul memories to emerge naturally because interesting parts such as visits to library or special activities could be missed. Interactive questions in the 'eternal now' with the elders and spirit guide are best left to the end to ensure that all the client's objectives have been fully met.

Blockages may occur in a spiritual regression. The most common come from clients who have difficulty entering deep trance. This is something that can be screened before a session, and reduced with the use of self-hypnosis CDs and experiencing past-life regression using hypnosis. The other blockage comes from the spirit guide either at the crossover into the spirit realms or later during part of the spiritual regression. Although this does not happen frequently it will always be for a reason. Normally it will be because the client will be working on some aspect of karma in their current-life and it is not the right time for them to know about those soul memories.

Sometimes analytical clients may wonder if the experience was 'real'. Some of the factors to help them decide include the spiritual intensity of reunions, the differences in some aspect of their regression from anything that they may have read and the level of visual detail that emerges. In deep hypnosis clients respond literally to questions, and unless there is conscious interference soul memories will emerge. Most importantly clients report there is an intuitive truth in the information that is relevant to their current life.

7

WORKING WITH BODY MEMORIES

The cure for pain is in the pain. Good and bad are mixed.
If you don't have both you don't belong to us.
Jelaluddin Rumi, 13th-century Sufi.

During a deep massage session many body workers have reported how past-life images often arise when a tense or a sensitive part of the body has been manipulated. It is as if they had 'tuned in' to some aspect of their energy field memories through the body. An example was a client who reported during a deep massage of his chest, an image of being pinned down by bodies. At a later point when more of the story emerged it appeared he had been a victim of the plague and was tipped into a pit with other bodies from a cart, but was still just alive.

Body memories can be created by one traumatic incident or accumulated over a period of time. A child who lives in fear of being hit by violent parents may learn to cringe, twist their head away and put their hands in the air in protection. If this continues, the threats of violence activate the muscles of the body until the muscles 'learn' this posture subconsciously. The child will be permanently on the alert so the fear remains locked in their organism together with chronically raised shoulders, twisted head, and tight nervous stomach. This holding pattern over the years can degenerate into a fixed posture[1]. The inability to resolve the situation results in a frozen body memory. Wilhelm Reich[2] called this body armor and went on to describe rigid patterns of unconscious muscular holding we find in the head, jaw, neck, shoulder, thorax, diaphragm, pelvis, legs, arms, hands and feet.

Many of the techniques used in this chapter are adapted from the work of Roger Woolger who has pioneered the use of past-life body awareness into regression therapy. He calls his approach *Deep Memory Processes*[3] and covers it in his books and articles[4]. In *Sensorimotor Psychotherapy* Pat Ogden and Dr Kekuni Minton[5] emphasize the importance of body memories, as does Tree Staunton[6] in the highly acclaimed book *Body Psychotherapy*. Appendix I discusses these and others in more detail.

LANGUAGE OF THE BODY

In the Western world there has been a culture of not showing feelings by repressing them. When this happens the body sensations accompanying the feelings also get blocked. As a result many people will find it difficult to describe their body sensations. Take a few minutes to think of as many words as possible to describe the sensations you could experience in your body.

The average person will list up to six. Examples of the sensation vocabulary include:

Pain, tension, freezing, trembling, vibrating, clammy, fuzzy, throbbing, flushed, tense, nauseous, heavy, dull, smooth, itchy, tight, tingly, sweaty, dense, faint, constricting, prickly, pressure, spinning, breathless, suffocating, sharp, locked, numb, shaky, moist, frantic, damp, cool, warm, bloated, dizzy, pounding, twitching, clamminess, tightness, and tingling.

Having a wider sensation vocabulary helps a person to deepen the awareness of their body state particularly when using a physical bridge. The therapist can help by encouraging a client to describe and locate their symptoms with the use of directional questions:

Is the sensation dull or sharp?

Is it throbbing or tight?

Is it near the surface or deep?

If a client is asked to describe sensations, they frequently do so with words such as 'panic' or 'fear', which refer to emotional states rather than to the sensation itself. When this occurs they can be asked to describe where in the body they hold it. Panic may be felt in the body as rapid heartbeat, trembling and shallow breathing. Anger might be experienced as a tension in the jaw or an impulse to strike out. Hopelessness might be experienced as collapse through the spine and a ducking of the head and shoulders.

EXPLORING BODY MEMORIES

For Sam her problem was created during a trip to Miami to see her son. One evening three armed men who were high on drugs had broken into their rented cottage and demanded money. She had her hands tied and was terrified of dying as a knife was thrust against her throat. She was kicked and had to endure watching her son and his wife beaten as she bravely refused to scream for fear of provoking the attackers. Sam had been having nightmares and panic attacks for 18 months and other therapies had not shifted the symptom:

She was asked to show the posture she was in when attacked. As her hands came together in front of her she started to sob as the memory came flooding back and was taken quickly through it. Reflecting back Sam said, '*I wanted to get the ropes off my wrists and shout at them but couldn't*'. She was asked to get into the posture again and a twisted towel was lightly wrapped round her wrists to recreate a psychodrama of the event. As she regressed into the memory she transformed it by forcing off the towel, and exploded in a torrent of shouting and curses. As she exhaled a smile came on her face. The panic attacks and nightmares left after the session.

Sam's complex started with the thought of her death, followed by the emotion of fear and then the body memories of hand posture and frozen scream. The transformation of her complex started with working with her body memories. These steps can be used to explore them. It starts with going to the point the complex started, which in the case of Sam was when her attack happened:

Go to the point just before ....

With body memories a client needs to be encouraged to *show* rather than *tell*.

Body show me what is happening.

Body show me what happens next.

Working with body memories often opens up a deep-seated catharsis, so care is needed not to overwhelm a client when it is released. With experience the therapist will know whether to allow it to be fully released or gradually over a number of a number regressions. Telling the body to go to the end repeatedly in a higher than normal voice is a way of controlling the cathartic release:

Body go to the end.

Working with body memories focuses the client on their body for the simple reason that it is here that the frozen body energy from a complex can be most effectively released and transformed. Therapy for the emotional and thought components of the complex can be done later.

TRANSFORMING PAST-LIFE BODY MEMORIES

Frequently, unexplainable physical symptoms in this life come from a violent past-life death. Hanging, battles, eaten by wild animals, torture, murdered, trapped by rocks, earthquake, rape, beaten by crowds are just a few or the deaths scenes that may be encountered. As Ian Stevenson identified from his research, the frozen physical memories from these events are so strong that they are often associated with inexplicable tension, pain and physical holding patterns in this life.

A case study that illustrates this is a client I will call Sally. She was in her late forties and had experienced chronic 'unexplainable pains' in the top of her spine and arms for as long as she could remember. She also had a history of disturbing thoughts of being alone. Sally had already had one regression therapy session in which she had regression into a past-life as a farmer's wife with a large family. The children had grown up and left the home one by one, and then her husband had been forced to leave home to find work elsewhere. She was left alone with little money or food and a young child of two she called 'baby'. The loneliness of that life had driven her to commit suicide. After resolving that past-life complex she was able to experience for the first time being truly happy in her own company. The second session was to work with her unexplainable pain:

Sally was asked to focus on the pain in her spine and was encouraged to adjust her posture. She sat upright with her hands in the air and regressed into the past-life of a ten-year-old girl about to have a red-hot poker held against the top of her spine as a punishment. Sally sobbed lightly and her body started to shake. The young girl was taken quickly through the death, which included falling to a cold dark floor to die in terror by herself. As the last breath was taken, Sally let out a sigh and her breathing slowed down.

The significant events of the past-life where reviewed. She had been happily living in London with her parents until they caught the plague. To stop her from catching it she was pushed out of the house and was told the neighbors would look after her. Unfortunately they suspected that she might be carrying the plague and was shunned, leaving her with nowhere to go except roam the cobble streets by herself. Survival was by stealing food and sleeping in cold doorways. She recalled smelling two large pies that had been put out to cool on the kitchen windowsill of a large house. With a desperate hunger she decided to take one of the pies but instead of running away, she sat down to eat it. A servant from the house caught her and called her a scruffy urchin who needed to be punished. Two men took her by the arms and eventually she was thrown into a dark dungeon. At a later point her arms were lifted up and tied to a beam forcing her legs just off the floor. Her scraps of clothing were ripped off and she became aware of another man heating a poker until it was red hot. She was taken quickly through the death.

The 'spine' and 'hands' were asked what they wanted to change from that past-life. Sally answered she wanted her hands freed and to push away the poker. The young girl was asked to go to the death point and into the body posture. As Sally sat up and lifted her arms upwards, a twisted towel was used as a prop to hold her hands. Hand pressure was applied to create the psychodrama of the poker. Sally described the pain in her spine and the smell of her burning flesh. She was encouraged to break her hands free and push away the poker by pushing against the therapist's steady hand pressure on her spine. She sighed with relief and reported that the pain and tension had completely gone from her spine.

In this case study the entry was in the middle of a violent death and she was quickly taken through it. The whole of the past-life was then reviewed. Because a physical bridge had been used the body memories at the complex point were known. Alternatively they could have been explored before their transformation. The transformation started by talking to the body 'parts' affected; her hands and spine. She was taken back to the past-life death point and allowed to physically experience removing the ropes that tied her and pushing away the red-hot poker. This very quickly transformed the frozen body memories from past-life, and Sally's 'unexplainable pain' in her spine and shoulder left at that point and have not troubled her since.

In a violent past-life death the client can to be taken quickly through the death point. This needs to be said with a raised voice and often repeated:

Go to the death point ... body go to the end.

Someone who was tortured may have a long and painful experience and death signals that the life is over. In reducing the duration of the death experience it may be necessary to repeat it. If a violent death is not fully remembered the client may not be aware of a scream that never come out, or a wound in their body that was not felt before. If there is resistance to dying perhaps because of a struggle or fight to live, it is important that this is remembered and released because this will be the source of a complex that is repeating in the current-life.

In line with the transformation in the spirit realms, its best to allow the client to decide how the change is to be experienced. When a body memory is being transformed the trauma is relived and each *part* brought to a new conclusion consciously. Talking to body parts helps focus on the different aspects of the transformation, and establishes if one or more psychodrama regressions will be needed. For example each body part could be a clenched fist, numb legs or bound hands:

Hands, (or arm, leg etc) **what do you want to do that you could never do?**

A shutdown complex can be spotted when a client is a victim in the middle of recounting a violent story and their body or legs become rigid. It can also manifest itself as a numbing of parts of the body, a dulling of inner body sensations and a slowing of muscular response. Because it involves a loss of vital energy, transforming frozen body parts needs extra energy. I personally find the use of Shaman power animals effective. When asked to find a spirit animal with the energy needed clients often report that they have come back with a lion, bear, tiger or something similar. The reality of what the energy is or where it comes from is less important than it seems to provide a metaphor to transform frozen limbs:

> **Go to the animal kingdom and find a spirit animal that has the energy you need … bring the animal energy inside you and feel the strength of the energy going inside** (fists, legs etc)

In the case of Sally the transformation started at the point just before she felt the hot poker:

> **Go to the point just before …**

Using props such as a towel or a cushion are helpful and can call for some creativity in their use. In the case study of Sally, pressure from the therapist's hand was used to create the effect of the poker so the body could experience pushing it away:

> **Body** (fist etc) **show me what you always wanted to do.**

Emotions, and in particular fear, act as a supercharger to build up enormous levels of energy that gets embedded with the body memories. When a blockage has been released there will be a natural flow of energy where it has not been before. Clients often emit a sigh or report sensations of warmth, trembling or new awareness in that part of their body.

TRANSFORMING CURRENT-LIFE BODY MEMORIES

When resistance or escape is impossible, the human system of self-defense becomes overwhelmed and disorganized. Examples are war situations, torture, sexual abuse and beatings in childhood. Sometimes called post-traumatic stress, these memories can be hyperactive complexes with symptoms of uncontrolled body spasms, aggression, hyper-alertness, and uncontrollable bouts of rage. Alternatively they can be shutdown complexes with symptoms of chronic patterns of submission, helplessness, inability to set boundaries, blocked feelings, numbness and a repetition of the victim role. Both complexes include panic attacks, nightmares, body pains and flashbacks.

A client I'll call Jo, was a 30-year-old single woman who had been diagnosed as suffering from post-traumatic stress. Her symptoms where stomach spasms, teeth chatter, difficulty breathing and a body shake which she constantly tried to contain. In her words *'It was as if my stomach and other parts of my body are not part of me, but separate living things'*. She also had trouble sleeping, often waking up at night in panic attacks. All these symptoms had been troubling her for ten years following a martial arts incident. In a poorly supervised training session her male opponent had gone into a rage and trapped her with his legs around her stomach and chest preventing her from breathing. Although she had no detailed memory of the events she remembered struggling desperately to be released and unable to say anything until she lapsed into unconsciousness. When she was revived she remembered the pain in her chest. The following day she discovered she had crushed ribs and had lost sensations in her hands and feet. The other symptoms appeared shortly afterwards. She had tried various traditional and complementary therapies over the years without relief:

Jo was invited to let her body show what happened at the event. She found it difficult at first to be aware of her body sensations because the hyper arousal of shaking, body arching, panic, and shouting became too overwhelming. Initially she was encouraged to trust her body by allowing the movements to occur without trying to direct them in any way but being able to stop at any moment if she felt it was too much. Allowing her to know this was important, since exposure to the traumatic event can be intense before it begins to unwind and soften. She was asked if she would be willing to experiment by feeling the pressure of a cushion on her stomach to experience the sensations of the legs that trapped her body. Jo consented and was encouraged to hold the cushion with her hands and push it away whenever the experience became too much. This put her in complete control. Initially her back arched and trembled as the cushion was pressed on her stomach and she immediately pushed it away. She was taken though the event slowly and asked to be aware of the sensations in her stomach. With each regression she was able to increase the duration before she pushed it away.

Jo asked to do some work with her throat and breathing difficulty. She was invited to breathe slowly and deeply as the cushion was pressed on her stomach. Initially she had difficulty and started to choke as she pushed away the pillow. With encouragement and several attempts her breathing became slower and deep. Jo still reported tension in her throat so she was asked to focus on these sensations in further regressions. Eventually she could breath steadily while experiencing the pressure of the cushion.

After 40 minutes of releasing and transforming the frozen body memories Jo was exhausted and allowed to savor the new body sensations. She reported feeling peaceful and more connected with her body.

Three more therapy sessions were needed working in a similar way on her stomach as well as her chattering teeth and shaking legs. The intensity levels in the sessions became increasing less but a residual level of body memory remained. Jo reported that it was easier sleeping now and she was less prone to flashbacks and spasms.

On the fifth session Jo reported that she wanted the session to focus on a relationship that she could not stop thinking about. This had finished around the same time as the martial arts event. With a sadness and longing in her heart, she regressed into a past-life of a medieval man. Jo reported a crushing sensation on her chest and lower body as she became aware of being at the bottom of a dark dry well with bodies being thrown on top of her one by one. The mediaeval man died a swift death and as he left the body Jo's breathing became easier and her body relaxed.

The past-life was reviewed. The man had been married to a young attractive dark-haired girl, and although they had been no children there was happiness and love. Some invaders had come from another part of the country and although he was only a simple farm worker the man was forced to join the defenders. Only armed with wooden weapons the defenders were no match for the invaders and he soon found himself overwhelmed and caught. Held by two soldiers he was pushed backwards into a well.

After the past-life death the mediaeval man was asked to meet the spirit of his wife and discovered that she was sad at losing him. Jo was given a cushion as a prop to hug and remembered the deep love the two had experienced. The mediaeval man was then asked to re-experience the death in the well and change it in any way the body needed. Wanting to stay with his wife, Jo was encouraged to keep holding the cushion as a reminder of the love between them. The mediaeval man was asked to go to the point when the first bodies were falling on him in the well. When pressure was applied to Jo's stomach she was able to continue holding the cushion. This was the first time Jo had been able to experience weight on her stomach without it triggering some reaction. A scan of Jo's body indicated all the tension had been cleared.

Following these sessions Jo reported her sleep pattern had now completely returned to normal with no panic attacks. She no longer had to consciously constrain her body, and her body felt as if it was whole. The suffering she had experienced in the dark well had fused with the traumatic martial arts event. By clearing the body memories from both events they reverberated into her present life. In her words '*I was a vegetable before, and now I have a second life and enjoy each moment to the full*'.

A hyperactive energy release like Jo's needs to be controlled so that the client on one hand can release and transform all the trapped energy and yet remain in control of what is happening. It needs to be done with great client sensitivity and with their full consent. The techniques of exploring and transforming frozen current-life body memories are the same as working with past lives, except that the level of energy is greater and it often takes more regression sessions.

PSYCHODRAMA

Sometimes a catharsis becomes stuck and is not released in the body therapy transformation. Psychodrama is a technique of building the tension of the event before the transformation by dramatizing it. For example, a complex may have started when a past-life slave was beaten but did not hit back. After obtaining the past-life story the client can be taken back to the point before the beating and the information about the situation used to create the tension. 'He's holding the stick ... It's about to hit you ... Notice your fist becoming clenched .... All the things you wanted to do but couldn't ... The stick coming down at any moment ... On the count of three …. One … Two … Remembering what happens to your body … Three.'

Breath and sound is another way of amplifying frozen feelings[7]. If a past-life character is angry and says, 'I want to hit him,' the therapist can match the volume of their voice, and encourage them to say it again and again. If they shout, the therapist can shout as well. This dramatizes the moment and intensifies the feelings. A person who is scared will take short breaths. If the therapist takes short quick breaths the sound of their breathing will also act as a model for the client. If a past-life character says they are sad and the emotions appear to be stuck, the therapist can say, 'Try taking long breaths and be aware what happens if you make the sound of sadness.'

DISSOCIATION AND FRAGMENTATION WITH DEEP TRAUMA

Dissociation of the mind from the body is a defense mechanism that allows a person to survive a fearful event without being trapped in the body to feel the physical pain. Consciousness seems to separate and leave the body, and the client will report seeing the event from a distance with no emotion or in a dream like state. In her book *The Process of Healing*, Alice Givens[8] noticed that clients can auto hypnotize themselves to avoid the trauma with thoughts of 'I don't want to feel this' or, 'It's not really happening'.

In extreme fear or terror this is taken further. Last century, Herman[9] highlighted in his work with hysteria that clients lost their capacity to integrate the memory of overwhelming life events. With careful investigative techniques he demonstrated that traumatic memories were preserved in an abnormal state, set apart and blocked from ordinary consciousness. Freud called the unresolved trauma a fixation, and Fairbairn one of the contributors to modern psychodynamic theory called it fragmentation[10]. It occurs during times of high emotional situations such as battlefield situations including wounds during battle, amputations, atrocities and torture. With repeated abuse over a period of time such as torture under interrogation or child abuse, multiple fragmentation occurs. If the memory fragment comes to conscious awareness at a later date some aspects of the emotional and physical symptoms associated with the event are recreated. For shell shock survivors who have been overwhelmed by fear in a battle situation this has been called a flashback. A noise may trigger a trembling of the body and intense fear. The fragment will not hold a clear story, just the thoughts at the time, pieces of emotion and body memories. If unresolved at death, the fragmented piece of consciousness is taken as a memory with the subtle body.

A case study that illustrates this is a client I'll call Rose. She was a mother in her forties whose major problem as presented in a public workshop, was that she had no sex drive with her husband. Whenever he penetrated her she would freeze up. Over the years she had inflicted self-harm on herself and was currently using smoking and drinking alcohol to numb herself from any feelings. Many years of conventional therapy had failed to deliver her from these complaints. Rose had little memory of her childhood, although six months previously she had an internal pelvic infection that had triggered a memory fragment of her father sexually abusing her, which was around the time that her asthma had started. She had the courage to share her very painful problem with the other therapists present at a workshop:

Rose regressed into a current-life memory of when she was eleven and looking out of a window as her father left, thinking, *'It was all my fault'*. She had found a tape of her father talking to his mistress and not fully understanding its content, had given it to her mother. Her mother had confronted her husband which resulting in him leaving home. As Rose repeated the words, *'It was all my fault'* she started to sob softly and was encouraged to change her body posture to go with the experience. Rose's lower body appeared rigid, and she reported numbness and a pressure. Images of boulders trapping her legs came, and as she explored the body memory of struggling to escape she let out a moan of frustration that turned into a cathartic release. Intuitively sensing this was a fragment of a past-life she was reminded that her poor body was dead and she could leave it now.

Rose was asked to recap the significant events. All she could remember was being a soldier in a battlefield and being trapped by falling rubble from a building. The soldier was taken back to the point when he first felt pressure on his legs from the rubble. A cushion was pressed onto Rose's legs and the soldier was encouraged to push off the rubble with the help of a 'spirit bear'. Rose started to cough and struggle for breath. More of the memory had surfaced and the soldier was breathing in dust from the falling building into his lungs. He was taken through the death again and Rose released more catharsis. Her body visibly relaxed at this point and her breathing returned to normal. The soldier was asked to recap the events from that life. He had been sent out to scout the enemy during World War 2 and being frightened to do this had given his leaders wrong information that led to many of them being slaughtered. He remembered the cannon shots, and the crows eating the corpses. The slaughter had been his fault. The therapist noted that giving information leading to a disaster was also a pattern related to Rose's childhood memory.

The soldier was asked to go back to the point when he first felt the rubble on his legs trapping him. He was encouraged to push the rubble away by pushing against firm pressure on a cushion held on Rose's legs and lower body. After the rubble had been pushed away Rose was asked to experience the sensations in her body. She stretched out her legs and felt them, and became aware that her breathing was easier. She was encouraged to move her legs and feel them moving and choose a running motion as she lay on her back. As her legs moved she became visibly relaxed and commented on how powerful she felt through her body as she was running.

Little Rose was asked if she had wanted to run away too. Rose's voice began to softly sob and her legs stopped moving as she recalled her childhood memory of feeling her father's weight crushing her. Little Rose was aware of leaving her body and looking down as her father abused her. A cushion was pressed on Rose's lower body and Little Rose was encouraged to push him off. As she pushed against the resistance of the cushion tears came to Rose's eyes and she sobbed and had difficulty breathing. She remembered the weight of her father was smothering her as she struggled to breathe. Initially she had no strength to push, but was encouraged to bring in the strength of the past-life soldier pushing off the rocks. As Little Rose pushed away her father and freed herself from the pressure she experienced energy flowing into her arms and chest. Little Rose was asked what her legs wanted to do, and allowed to express this with Rose moving her legs in a running motion. As she experienced feelings coming back to her lower body little Rose became confused because she was remembering the pleasure from her genitals at the time. She was reminded that everyone's genitals automatically respond in that way, and was given a helpful thought to say of, *'I don't blame you having pleasure genitals, what you were doing was natural and normal'*. As she integrated the genital memory fragment Roses face became more relaxed.

Little Rose remembered her father telling her that the police would take her away if she told her mother. She was given permission to visualize her mother and say the words she always wanted to say. Tears came to Rose's eyes as she told her mother what her father had done to her. She was asked to scan her body for any tension, and indicated that her legs still felt tight. Rose was encouraged to let her legs feel the running motion again as she breathed deeply. A smile came to her face as she said she was really enjoying doing it now.

What this case demonstrates is that it is possible to work through quite severe trauma very effectively, providing the whole body is engaged. When fully encouraged, physical and emotional release, and fragment integration can be accomplished very swiftly. In cases of painful childhood memories, past lives are a back door to release frozen memories before a current-life trauma is processed. Painful as it may have looked to an observer, it was actually a huge relief for Rose as everyone in the workshop could observe from the way she looked and talked about it after the work. After this session Rose was able to stop her self-harm, and decide to give up smoking and drinking alcohol. She found she could connect with her emotions even though some were still painful, and with further regression therapy sessions she released other memories associated with four years of abuse by her father. After several therapy sessions her sex life improved and her asthma cleared.

In more complex cases of multiple fragmentation each fragment may be associated with a different traumatic event. In this case each fragment and traumatic memory will need to be identified and processed. The strategy when working with current- or past-life fragmentation is to bring the fragmentation memory to the client's conscious awareness and then integrate it with the rest of the client's actions in the transformation.

SUMMARY

This type of work brings about the most amazing healing of chronic complexes. However, the high levels of energy released means it needs to be done with great client sensitivity and their full consent. As illustrated with the case study of Jo's post-traumatic stress, frozen energy locked in the body may need to be released and transformed over a number of sessions. The therapist should follow the flow of energy wherever it goes. Sometimes a past-life is an entry point to a childhood trauma that is too painful to face without first discharging some of the energy as illustrated with Rose's case study. Often current-life experiences are a bridge into the origins of the complex in a past-life. Release and transforming the frozen body memories is the first priority by allowing the client to go back to the trauma point and completing it in a different way. The case studies illustrate how allowing the affected body parts to find completion with the creative use of props can transform physical body memories.

Dissociation and fragmentation often occur with violent memories. The client needs to be embodied at the point before the event happened. Encouraging body movement helps to keep the client focused on their body. The focus is 'show me' rather than 'tell me'. Each fragment body memory needs to be integrated into the whole body by bringing consciousness into that area.

8

INTRUSIVE ENERGY

The nature of everything is illusory and ephemeral.
How pitiful they who cling strongly to concrete reality.
Turn your attention within my friends.
Nyoshul Khenpo.

From the previous chapters I have illustrated how souls split their energy before incarnating and how the incarnated part can become earthbound. Eventually this soul energy will return to the spirit world and be reunited with the rest of the soul.

BACKGROUND

Can this earthbound soul energy become attached to people in this life? The subtle body is designed to protect us from energies other than our own. When our protection is down, energy can be accumulated into our current-life in the form of negative thoughts and emotions. When it comes to soul energy attachments the pioneers who have done most work in the area are William Baldwin who wrote the book *Spirit Releasment Therapy*[1] and Louise Ireland-Frey in her book *Freeing the Captives*[2]. They take the position that the spiritual energy not following the normal path of going to the spirit realms often contains unresolved traumatic memories. This is attracted to living people with similar problems in a form of a psychic resonance. It can be a particular desire such as violence, suffering, or an addiction to drink or drugs. Alternatively it may identify with a particular emotion such as anger, depression or guilt. Sometimes it may just want companionship and is drawn to the compassion of the host. It can attach itself to a person's energy field after it has been weakened by events such as life traumas, accidents, operations, excessive drinking or drug taking. An example of this is drawn from William Baldwin's book, *Spirit Releasment Therapy*:

> Gerry was in his forties and worked for a US city fire department. He was the first to reach a lakeside dock where a drowning victim had been pulled from the water. He applied mouth-to-mouth resuscitation and was angry when it was to no avail. Gerry then behaved differently than he normally did in such circumstances. He walked to the hospital where the body had gone and tried to get through the doors in the emergency treatment room to where the body had been carried. He felt a powerful compulsion just to stay close to it. Other aspects of his life deteriorated too. Not until the spirit of the drowned boy was released from him did it become clear what had happened. His strong negative feelings of anger had opened a chink in his normal protection.

This view on spirit attachment is controversial. Michael Newton reports that in over 30 years of research he has never had a client during a spiritual regression that has reported having a spirit attachment from another spirit, friendly or otherwise. His clients have talked about the existence of an abundance of negative energy from others people's intense emotions of anger, hate and fear which has been attracted to negative thinkers. Dolores Cannon in her book *Between Death and Life*[3] has some client

174

reports that spirit attachment occurs but only when there is an imbalance in the host's energy field. However, one of her clients reported that all suspected spirit attachments are negative energies that have been attracted to them.

In the world of regression therapy the pioneers Hans TenDam and Roger Woolger both work with spirit attachments. Alan Sanderson a retired psychiatrist from England and founder of the Spirit Release Foundation[4] takes the view that many mental health problems are associated with spirit attachments. Other regression therapists take the position of Michael Newton or go further and suggest this whole area is the result of a client's sub personalities from unresolved trauma becoming linked to vivid fantasies.

I find that sometimes clients have inner world experiences that appear to be spirit attachments or powerful negative thought forms that they have attracted. Collectively I call this intrusive energy. By treating it as this, the framework of clearing becomes quick and many unwanted behaviors and emotional symptoms are either reduced or removed. Before, or during regression therapy intrusive energy can be encountered and it needs clearing in the process of working with a client's complex. This chapter is not intended to be fully comprehensive but sufficient for practical use with most forms of intrusive energy commonly encountered. For those wanting more in-depth information I recommend William Baldwin or Louise Ireland-Frey books mentioned earlier from which I have selectively used or adapted their techniques.

DETECTION

A standard muscle-testing technique from kinesiology can be used. Muscles will be become weak in the presence of something that is stressing the energy system. Gentle pressure can be applied to a muscle such as a bent arm and the client asked to resist the pressure. All that is needed is to say the words of the test and the arm will go down if this is stressing the energy system. However, intrusive energy can sometimes 'scramble' the energy system so that the correct muscle response is not always given. To prevent this from happening it is important to ask for the client's higher self to have control over the muscle responses to prevent interference.

Those unfamiliar with kinesiology can use finger signals similar to those used in hypnosis as an alternative technique to communicate with the client's higher mind. With the client reclined following an energy scan or light trance, the following steps will facilitate this type of finger signal:

I want to communicate to your higher mind through your fingers. Just let your conscious mind drift to the background.

Let your higher mind lift a finger to be your right hand to be your 'Yes finger'. Wait for a finger to lift. **Good.**

Let your higher mind lift another finger to be your hand to be the 'No finger'. Wait for a finger to lift. **Good.**

It is useful to check by asking a question with an obvious yes and no answer. The presence of intrusive energy can then be detected using the fingers to indicate the answer. The following questions can be asked, waiting for the response and them acknowledging it:

Is there any energy that does not belong with you?

Are there 2 (or 3, 4 etc) **or more energies?**

Is there exactly 1 (or 2, 3 etc) **energy?**

Another technique that can be used is the energy scan discussed in the previous chapters. However, the intention now needs to be to look for energy not belonging to the client:

> **I'm going to scan for any energy that does not belong with you. With your eyes closed focus on the area around your body as my hand move slowly several inches from your body from your toes to your head. Tell me the part of the body that feels lighter or heavier or different in any way.**

While the scan is underway the client can be encouraged to focus on different areas:

> **I'm scanning the energy around your feet ... lower legs ... knees ...**

The scan may need to be repeated two or three times, because each one increases the sensitivity for both the therapist and client. Those therapists new to this work may prefer to use two different techniques to be quite sure that they have identified intrusive energy.

RELEASING SPIRITS ATTACHMENTS

Once energy has been detected it can be encouraged to talk through the client. A case study that illustrates this is a client I'll call Lena. When she told me her life story it was hard not to feel sorry. She had been abandoned by her mother at birth, and brought up by her grandmother who had died when she was six. Her boyfriend left her when she was pregnant at sixteen forcing her into an abortion. Then in her early twenties her long-time boyfriend left her. She had been in and out of depressions and had tried to commit suicide twice. She was currently working as a professional dancer:

> As Lena was being scanned she was able to detect an area round her legs that felt heavier, and did not seem to belong to her. As she focused on the area Lena was encouraged to let the energy talk through her and say the first thought that entered her mind. She suddenly said, *'Victoria'*. In the dialogue it was reported that Victoria was a seven-year-old girl in a red dress with a white ribbon. Having been pushed off her rocking horse by her brother she had died from a blow to her head in the fall. She was upset that no one had taken any notice of her. Victoria was attracted to Lena during a time when she had been sobbing in her bedroom in a deep mood of depression. Victoria had always wanted to be a dancer and explained that she was able to fulfill her longing to dance whenever Lena was dancing. Lena was initially reluctant to release Victoria because she would have had a little girl of her own if she had not had an abortion earlier in her life. Through further questioning of Victoria it was quickly found that she would be willing to leave Lena to be reunited with the spirit of a loving child minder. As Victoria was released Lena commented on feeling lighter as she left. She also explained that over the last few months following her depression she had thought a number of times that someone was with her. A scan confirmed that Lena's energy blockage had cleared following the release of Victoria. The rest of the session focused on Lena's current-life problems.

Victoria had all the appearance of a spirit that had become earth bound and had attachment itself to Lena when her energy field was weakened during her depression. It did not seem to have had any detrimental effect on Lena except an awareness of a presence that left following the session. It was treated in a compassionate way and helped back to the spirit realms.

For multiple attachments I usually start with the strongest. This can be established with client feedback during the scan or with a finger signal. Then contact can be made:

Allow your conscious mind to drift to the background, knowing you will be safe and protected in the session. I want you to allow the energy in your chest (legs etc.) **to move to your throat and speak to me.**

Hello, my name is (therapists name) **what's your name?**

Sometimes a little perseverance is needed to get a name. Once it is given there usually no delay in finding out more about it. Most appear to be glad to converse with someone. Further information such as sex, age, and personality details can be gathered. In the dialogue with a spirit attachment it is important to ensure that it realizes that it is dead. This may require taking it to the last moments before its death, and allowing it to re-experience how it died. Also important is to find out what was happening in the client's life when it attached. This may be an emotional 'hook' that will require clearing in later regression therapy. Many questions can be asked depending on the answer to the previous question. Possible questions include:

What was happening in (the client's) **life when you joined him/her?**

What your life was like when you had your own body?

What happened when you died?

Historical or biographical details are less important than getting to the core issue of what is needed for it to be released the spirit realms. This could be by being reunited with a loved one from its past-life or a child minder for babies:

When you died what stopped you going to the spirit realms?

If we find your loved one will you be willing to leave for the spirit realms to join them?

When the attachment is ready to leave the client can be asked to help push it out. They may describe sensations such as tingling, feeling lighter, or an awareness of something leaving them. One client said, 'Something just stood up and left me'. The release needs to be repeated for each attachment, although for multiple attachments the final ones can be invited to leave together:

Imagine a net of light being dragged along your body collecting all the energies not belonging to you and being taken to the light.

CLEARING NEGATIVE INTRUSIVE ENERGY

We all have thoughts in our head, but when they become voices that take a life of their own it may indicate a spirit attachment with negative energy. It illustrate this I'll use the case study of a client I'll call Joe, a Nigerian living and working in Germany. For two years he had been hearing voices speaking to him in his head. They told him to do bad things to people and he was becoming more and more tormented fighting these 'commands', and the intense anger created inside him when they spoke. His wife had left him because she was afraid and by the time he came for the session he was feeling very low and exhausted. Joe had seen his doctor for help and following a visit to a psychiatrist was prescribed drugs to help with the hallucinations. The drugs made no difference and Joe was becoming more and more isolated:

> Working with the usual technique of speaking to the intrusive energy through the client proved impossible. Firstly there was the language barrier because Joe's English was poor, and also he was very anxious and wanted to keep talking about how this energy was affecting him. A simple relaxation technique was used which quickly subdued him. This allowed time for his energy field to be scanned. The intrusive energy was powerful, and Joe wanted it to go but thought it would not leave willingly. He started to feel anxious as he became more aware of the energy so the therapist spoke out loudly, "*I call on the Spirits of Light to remove this energy*". Joe began to feel safe as the process was outlined of how the spirits were going to remove it. He was also asked to visualize what was happening to all this negative energy. He said, '*It's being enveloped in light and taken away from me'.* Joe's higher self then confirmed that it was gone and that there was also no other intrusive energy with him. He was given healing energy to his subtle body and at the end of the session was incredibly calm, and said he felt as though a huge stone had been lifted off his chest.

In the case of Joe it was not possible to enter into dialogue because of his poor language skills and agitated condition. Even with good language skills this type of intrusive energy is often difficult to work with. Hans TenDam calls it an 'Obsessor'. Whether the technique can be described as creative visualization or the release of a negative spirit attachment is less important than Joe's voices and negative feelings stopping the moment he sat up after the session. In a follow-up call a month later he was totally at peace with himself and was working at putting his marriage back together again.

A client may have low energy levels or changed behaviors following some trauma, death, miscarriage or an operation. Another clue is when a client says, 'It's as if another part of me is laughing'. Intrusive energy can show up in the middle of therapy and can be indicated by a sensation that seems to change location during a session, such as from the shoulder to the head and then to the back.

Many spirit attachments may not be aware of the type of host body they are with. A male one was amazed to discover he was in the petite body of a young girl with breasts:

Do you realize this is not your rightful body?

They can be asked to bring in a tiny spark of love inside them. Often they will report that the light is growing in size and brightness until they are transformed and are then ready to leave the client:

Bring a spark of pure love into the centre of you. What starts to happen?

These sessions don't follow any set process and intuition with a little creativity may be needed. Completion is when the attachment has been released to the spirit realms.

The case of Joe illustrates how getting a response to questions from stronger energies may be difficult. Sometimes communication will be restricted to finger signals or the help of spirits of light that specialize in working with lost spirits. Michael Newton calls them 'Redeemers of Lost Souls'[5]. From the spirit realms they help lost spirits on the earth plane to cross over into the spirit realms. Personally I always invite a spirit guide to assist in guiding a released spirit attachment to the spirit realms. This way it ensures that departing energy does not come back:

I ask for a spirit of light to come and take this energy to the light.

In the case study of Joe, I need to thank Di Griffiths[6] a regression therapist and trainer who specializes in working with intrusive energy for supplying the case study.

Sometimes the intrusive energy may appear to be a negative thought form:

Have you ever had a human body of your own?

If the answer to this question is 'no', the dialogue with the negative energy can still continue. This is similar to dialogue with 'parts' used by many hypnotherapists. If negative energy is regressed back to the point when it first joined the client there will often be a description of the client's emotions or problems at the time. I prefer to work with this using regression therapy:

Go back to the point when (the attachment) **first joined you and tell me what is happening?**

A special form of negative energy is a curse. Created by intense focused thought, much of its effect may be fuelled by a client's fear. Because an energy link exists between the person who asked for the curse to be sent, the person who sent it, and the client, an intuitive dialogue between them similar to spirit realms encounters can be used. This gives the client new insights and understanding.

Spirit guides can be called to assist and help in dissolving the energy link.

PROTECTION AND DEBRIEF

At the end of a session the client's energy field will need energy added and balancing. If the therapist has been trained in channeling energy a finger test can be used to check how much energy is needed:

Let your higher mind lift the 'yes' finger when your energy field has been healed.

Clients can do it themselves. The first step is to make their intent clear to bring energy from the higher self to any part of their energy field that needs to be filled. The next is to visualize or feel white light being drawn down the head charka and then wrapped around the body from the head to the feet like a bandage. Several breathing cycles can be used to build up the energy.

At the end of the session the client will want to know what happened and may need reassurance. Hollywood horror films and religious exorcisms have influenced the popular perception of a spirit attachment, and some clients may be fearful. I sometimes explain that they have been the host of an unwelcome visitor that has lost its way, and explain how the energy became attached when their normal defences were down. An analogy is the physical body that has lots of parasites and bacteria that are invisible to the eye, and it only when they cause a problem that they need to be dealt with. The best protection is to clear complexes to make us less vulnerable. Sometimes I explain the therapy as imaginative visualisation and dialogue with 'parts', which is a form of psychotherapy. Also that discussing the experience outside the therapy session will be unhelpful because friends and others will often not understand. All that is important is the therapeutic benefit for the client.

SUMMARY

Intrusive energy is a controversial subject and may be seen by some as discrediting the professional position of regression therapy. I have only included it after a lot of thought because I think it is important and presents another facet of working with soul energy. I personally find I only need to work with it occasionally, although some of my colleagues may use it more frequently. Clues about intrusive energy come from the client interview, blockages or sensations that appear to move for no logical reason. Energy scans and finger testing can confirm if it is present and for those more sensitive intuition can be used. No one approach will be right for all clients and an important step is getting into dialogue with the spirit attachment through the client. In the case of negative attachments this may be more difficult and perseverance may be needed.

Finding out what stopped the attachment going to the spirit realms and what it needs to leave is important information to collect. Often loved ones from the past-life or specialist spirit minder for babies are all that is needed, and going to the light signals completion. Many client symptoms reduce with the departure of intrusive energy and previous blockages entering into hypnosis or a past-life often disappear. Asking what was happening in the client's life when the attachment occurred allows any emotional hook to be identified and cleared with later regression therapy. At the end a session the client will need an explanation of what happened. The depth of truth is less important than it sounds logical and coherent.

9

INTEGRATION

When the mind is a peace, the world too is at peace.
Nothing real, nothing absent.
Not holding on to reality, not getting stuck in the void.
You are neither holy nor wise,
just an ordinary fellow completing the work.
Layman P'ang 8th- century Chinese Zen Master.

Experiencing the past-life or current-life memories enables a person to understand the cause of their problem. The spirit realm encounters give new understandings, and frozen energy from the origin of complexes can be released and transformed. Afterwards the experience needs to be fully integrated into a client's present life to complete the healing process.

INTEGRATING A PAST-LIFE REGRESSION

The simplest way of integrating a past-life into the current-life is by asking about the patterns between them. To illustrate this I'll use the case study of a client I'll call Jenny. The tension on her facial expression was obvious as she described the reason for coming for therapy, *'It's not easy for me to say, it's about a physical aspect of my relationship'*. Despite several years of counseling and other therapies something was still wrong:

Jenny regressed into the past-life of a seven-year-old girl working as a maid in a large house. She had dropped a porcelain figurine that she had been trying to steal. It had shattered on impact with the floor and she was desperately trying to pick up the pieces. Jenny started to make choking sounds and said, *'My throat, I'm being strangled'*. The little girl was quickly taken though the death. Her dying thought was, *'I was trying so hard. I wasn't good enough'*.

The little girl was asked to recap the significant events of that live. She had been sent to work in the big house by her parents without understanding the reason. After arriving she was presented to the master and his family and at this point became aware of the teenage son looking her up and down with an evil sneer on his face. All the staff knew he had a temper so she tried to avoid him. At a later point she stole a valuable porcelain figurine by hiding it in her skirt. Unfortunately the son had gabbed her arm as she passed and the porcelain figurine had dropped to the floor and shattered. As she bent down to try and pick up the pieces he positioned himself over her, and she could hear his angry monotone voice. He had used a leather strap he was carrying to choke her to death.

In the spirit realms the little girl had a reunion with the spirits of her mother and father and in the dialogue found the reason for being sent to the house to work. Although they loved her, with little money or food they had no choice. Realizing this Jenny visually relaxed as she said the words, *'I am good enough'*. When the little girl met the spirit of the son who had strangled her she wanted to show him that the porcelain figurine was not broken. With the aid of a prop she had an emotional encounter presenting the figurine back to him saying, *'It's not broken. Look after it'*. Then she smiled saying, *'And don't kill anyone else for it!'*

In a body scan Jenny reported that she still felt tension on the side of her head. She was regressed to the point the tension first started which was trying to pick up the pieces of the shattered figurine. With intuitive inspiration Jenny said, *'I don't need to look frantically. It's OK for the pieces just to be there'*. She was asked if there was some pattern from the little girl trying frantically to put the pieces together with her current-life. Tears swelled in her eyes and a tissue was offered. *'I'm trying to fix the sexual side of life with my husband but cannot'*. She was asked how the little girl released the pressure from her head. Jenny said, *'By stopping giving herself such a hard time'*. Suddenly Jenny laughed, *'I don't need to give myself a hard time anymore. I am good enough'*. She was given this as an affirmation to take in her current-life.

Two weeks after the session Jenny sent the following email:

'Within my relationship I feel much more relaxed in general. I had always felt quite antagonized but that has completely gone and I am able to laugh about things much more. I believe the porcelain figure [from the session] *was symbolic of the relationship, which I felt I destroyed and could never be fixed. I now feel reassured and all doubts have gone. Using the affirmation, 'I am good enough,' has been very powerful. Whenever I had a problem and felt downhearted I used the affirmation and felt much more relaxed. I feel less of a child being smothered. I'm more of a capable person who can do anything, and is good enough. Words don't express my eternal gratitude.'*

For Jenny the pattern between the past-life and her current-life was the thought of not being good enough. For other clients it may be an emotion, physical sensation, relationship issue or even recognizing a person:

Do you recognize any patterns from that life being worked out in this life?

Do you recognize any of the people from past-life working out in this life?

Still in an altered state of awareness there may be a pause until intuitive insights appear. If some pattern has been missed a suggestion can be made, 'Is there any pattern between the pain in your back in the past-life and your current-life?' Probing questions to prompt the client's self-discovery are more powerful than offering views or opinions.

When a client has had symptoms with negative obsessive thoughts I like to agree with them an affirmation to take into their current-life. The affirmation should be focused at creating a positive statement from the dying thought or from the obsession. In the case of Jenny her dying thought of, 'I was trying so hard, I'm not good enough' was changed into an affirmation, 'I am good enough'. Affirmations are a way of countering the negative thoughts that have 'bled through' into the current-life from the past-life. When the charge associated with an obsessive thought has been removed during the regression, it is easier for a reinforcing cycle of positive self-talk to be created.

Self-Talk

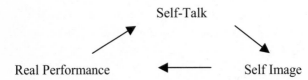

Real Performance   ←   Self Image

The affirmation needs to be worded in the present tense, be positive, and appeal to the imagination or emotions rather than the intellect. Examples are, 'I am strong as I stand up to men' or 'I take pleasure in guiding my own destiny'. They can be repeated regularly or written on a card in a prominent place to remind the conscious mind.

After a spiritual regression it is useful to summarize the order of events such as the past life review and meeting the soul group. Probing questions can be asked on the content:

What key aspects do you remember about this part and in what way was it helpful?

I advise that they wait for a few weeks before listening to the recording. Every time the CD is played further insights are possible because of the amount of information contained in them. After they have had time for reflection I ask for a summary of how the information has helped to be emailed or posted to me. This assists the integration process.

INTEGRATING REGRESSION THERAPY

In regression therapy the timeline is extended to include current-life significant events as well as those from a past-life that are related to the client's problem. All of them need to be brought to conscious awareness and transformed over one or multiple sessions. A case study of a client I'll call Jane can be used to illustrate this. She was 32 and a mother of two small boys and a girl. Currently she was living with her boyfriend and had a job as a night nurse. Two years previously she had become mildly depressed following a separation with her husband. She had a chronic pattern of abuse in relationships and had hung on to the relationship with her husband even though he had a bad temper. Anxious about her current boyfriend leaving, she had seen various therapists and was aware of her issues but found it difficult to put them into action. Recently she was experiencing panic attacks two or three times a day accompanied with spasms and pains in her stomach. She was off sick from work and her doctor had offered to double her medication, but she wanted to try a different approach:

Almost a soon as Jane talked about her last panic attack the previous evening her stomach started to spasm. When she was asked to focus on it, her neck and jaw tightened and eventually her whole body was shaking. When the intensity had subsided she was asked to bring up an image related to these sensations. She talked about a memory of a caesarean operation ten years previously. Under local aesthetic she was cut open and terrified that her baby was going to die, but was unable to move. Regressed back to the memory, Jane was encouraged to bend forward and visualize looking at the healthy baby.

Focusing on the residual tension in her stomach Jane regressed to an earlier current-life memory. She was five years old and in a small wooden boat used for holiday sightseeing. A sudden squall had blown up and the water started coming over the side of her boat. Her father was at the other end of the boat and thinking she was going to die, she had cried clinging to the leg of the nearest man. This was made worse when her father laughed at the sight of his daughter holding a stranger's leg. Unfortunately he did not realize the traumatic event she was experiencing. Jane was asked to let her body show what was happening. As she adjusting her body position and sat upright grasping hard at a cushion, her whole body started shaking and her breath became shallow and rapid. When this had settled she was allowed to change any aspects she wanted. As she regressed back again she shouted at her father, *'I need you. You have no right to laugh at me'.* Following further transformation regressions she was able to recall the memory without experiencing a panic attack.

A major focus of this session was working with the body memories from two traumatic incidents in Jane's earlier life. With the intense release in this type of session care was made to work carefully within what Jane could cope with in a single session. Jane came for her second session one week later. She reported that the panic attacks and spasms had reduced in frequency and intensity. She wanted to do more work on the spasms:

As she talked about her last panic attack Jane's stomach stared to shake. She was asked to focus on her stomach sensations and go to the point when they first started. Her whole body started to shake, and she gasped, *'All the air's going. I'm being squeezed. Oh my stomach. There's a group of natives closing in. One has a knife and I can feel his body. Oh the knife is going into my stomach'.* She was taken quickly through the death.

Jane reviewed the past-life in more detail. She had been a pregnant Victorian woman who had been washed overboard during a storm on a sailing ship. Close to drowning she had eventually swam ashore and found her self on the beach surrounded by native women and children. They looked after her and eventually she gave birth to twin boys. Some time later while walking alone a group of native men approached her. As she backed against a tree one of them attacked her and eventually stabbed her in the stomach. As she took her last breath she recalled leaving her body, floating up and seeing her body in the distance below. Her dying thoughts were about not seeing her children again.

She was regressed to the point before she felt the pain from being stabbed and encouraged to change it in any way she wanted. With the aid of a cushion as a prop she was allowed to experience pushing the native away, and pulling out the knife by pushing against the therapist's hand pressure. With a sigh, Jane reported that the pain in her stomach had gone and she felt calm.

In the spirit realms the Victorian woman was invited to meet her children and find out what had happened to them. With a surprised voice she said, *'They're sorry at what happened to me'*. A cushion was used for her to experience the reunion of hugging. Next was the native who had killed her. With the support of her children she discovered he was sorry and asked for forgiveness. Through the intuitive encounter she realized that the native who abused her had a wife and children in the village that were dependent on him. By forgiving him she was also forgiving the native's wife and children too. Even though this had been an intense session she felt a great relief at the release she had experienced.

Probing and awakening these different memories can be like peeling skins from an onion. By following the energy various layers of memory emerged until the frozen memories associated with a complex are available to be released and transformed. An important part of this session was helping Jane to find understanding and forgiveness in the past-life. Many people often find it easier to forgive in a past-life before they are ready to do the same in their present-life. This was the content of Jane's third session. After the last past-life was discussed she was regressed into her current-life memories that had the same pattern of being a victim:

Jane recounted the memories of abuse from her boyfriend and ex husband. She was asked to imagine meeting her ex husband and saying what she was never able to say at the time. After a deep pause she said, *'I cannot live with your temper. It's not right for the children'.* She was asked to imagine his reply, which was he had a temper because of stress of work and could not cope with Jane's temper either. The therapist reminded Jane how she had found forgiveness in the past-life, which helped her come to a resolution. She then had an emotional hug with her ex husband with the help of a cushion. A similar process followed with her boyfriend. Jane was now ready to confront her boyfriend even if he left, which was a brave new step for her.

Just understanding the patterns between a past-life and the current-life is often sufficient for integration. However, when emotional charges from the current-life are still present they need to be released and a resolution found. Sometimes this can be done in one session or over a number. In her first session Jane resolved issues with her father and in the third session worked with her ex husband and current boyfriend. I have illustrated how in past-life regression an intuitive link exists between attached emotional energy and other past-life characters. In an altered state of awareness dialogue can take place using this intuitive link. The same principals apply to the attached emotional energy from someone in this life:

Allow yourself to connect with (the current-life person). **What do you want to say to them that you could never say at the time? What do they say to you?**

Transformational dialogue and new insights and forgiveness can come from these meetings.

BALANCING ENERGY AND GROUNDING

Often regression sessions can be intense when frozen body energy has been released. Clients who have had a deep body massage find that toxins are often released into the blood and the following few days may experience very mild flu like symptoms. When there has been a deep energy blockage or a spirit attachment released, similar symptoms occasionally are experienced until the energy field is settled. This simply indicates that the healing process is taking place, and clients can be informed of this so they are not surprised.

To assist in balancing the energy field at the end of a regression session many therapists take a few minutes to channel energy to the client's energy field before they leave. This can be done quickly by using reiki, touch therapy, spiritual healing or a similar energy technique. Some regression therapists think that adding energy from outside is not needed and it is best for clients to be taught to do it themselves. The white light techniques mentioned earlier can be used. I think there is merit in both approaches and only channel energy myself for a short time if I'm intuitively drawn to do it. Also a bath can assist in cleansing the energy field. I advise that the client is gentle with themselves for the next 24 hours and avoid any emotional situation.

After the deep hypnosis in a spiritual regression, time will be needed to allow for a client to come back to a wide-awake state. It also allows the blood circulation to increase back to normal. A count down from ten to one can be used while encouraging motion in different part of the physical body. This is much more gentle than quickly sitting in an upright sitting position.

196

Even if hypnosis is not used an alternative state of awareness occurs naturally as part of the process of focusing on inner world experiences. It is important for the client to become fully grounded and 'in the body'. Some activities like driving a car can be dangerous because concentration on the road will be affected. Grounding can start at the end of session by allowing ten minutes of discussion while sitting in an upright posture. Other grounding activities include having a drink of water and going for a long walk.

OTHER INTEGRATION ACTIVITIES

With childhood trauma writing a letter from the inner-child to the older-self is a powerful way of integrating the output of a regression session. This letter from a client I'll call Sonia captures her reoccurring problem from childhood. Notice the delicate wording she uses which must have taken considerable time in choosing them:

I was a beautiful child so carefree and happy. A loving family brought me up with a desire to please. Then from about the age of ten evil conspired to never make me the same again. *'It's our little secret'*, he said. *'They wouldn't understand. You're my special girl. I love you'*. As I felt his hands it didn't feel right but I couldn't stop it happening. I was trained well to lead a life of secrets, lies and shame. Aged 13, a teenager feigning happiness but carefree, my childhood memories blocked in order to protect me. *'You're so beautiful'* he said, *don't tell anyone'*. It was different hands but the same secrets, lies and shame. Now 18 and pretty, but lacking self-respect, the pregnancy wasn't planned. But what could I expect, certainly not an abortion, but I did as my mother bid. She was determined I would not ruin my life like she did. I grew up and fell in love, but the man had hands. Beaten and raped I believe no one would understand. Through physical, emotional and mental torture, I was put to the test. I passed with flying colors, I'd been taught by the best. A nervous breakdown they said, depression showed its hand, suicidal thoughts, so much anger and so much pain. Still working on other feelings, but now no more secrets, lies or shame.

Words have a powerful and moving effect. If the healing is still incomplete and the client has been a victim, the memory may still be too painful to confront an abuser. Writing provides some level of dissociation. Penny Parks[1] who has spent her life working with adults who were sexually abused as children writes in her important book *Rescuing the Inner Child* the importance of integrating the 'inner-child' through drawings and writing letters about the experience.

With victims of child abuse many clients have grown up emotionally crippled by a huge burden of self-disgust. Many find it difficult to form a mature sexual and trusting relationship. As discussed in the case study of Rose in the previous chapter a past-life is often a backdoor before these painful childhood memories can be faced.

Activities between regression sessions can continue the process of integration and provide self-empowerment in the healing process. Writing a log of each past-life helps, and further insights over the following days or weeks can be added. Those who have experienced dissociation can be encouraged to do physical activities such as horse riding, fencing, football or any sport that associates consciousness with the body. A client unable to express a frozen scream can be asked to do an activity involving shouting such as a white-knuckle ride with their children. Relationship issues may need to be resolved by using the insights from the regression.

At the beginning of every session the therapist can review these activities. Questions to the client on symptom reduction will enable a therapist to get feedback on the previous session outcome. Although remarkable progress can be made in one session, it is best to initially plan for around three sessions or with deep complexes five.

SUMMARY

After a regression, the experience needs to be fully integrated into a client's present life to complete the healing process. Just understanding the patterns between a past-life and the current-life is often sufficient. These can be patterns such as abandonment, loneliness, being a victim, or reoccurring emotion and physical symptoms. The patterns can also be intuitively spotting past-life characters working out in the present life. For a single therapy session feedback is needed from the client via a phone call or email, and probing questions can continue the integration process.

For many complexes the regressing needs to cover some combination of past-life and current-life memories. Often a past-life is a back door to partially heal painful current-life memories before they can be faced. These can then be treated in the same way as significant past-life events, and intuitive encounters with the other people involved can be facilitated. In an altered state of awareness new insights and completion can come from these encounters. Other integration activities include past-life journals, inner-child writing assignments and working through relationship issues.

10

INTERVIEW

Everyone knows we have complexes,
but what people forget is that complexes have us.
Carl Jung.

I picked up the phone one day and this is an extract of the conversation:

Can you give a past-life regression for my son. Well ...
daughter if he goes ahead with a sex change operation.
He's on hormone medication and has changed his name to
Mary. I'm at my wits end because he won't talk about it to
anyone. He's going to Holland for the surgery in a few
months' time.
Does he ... she ... want a past-life regression?
Yes, but he won't speak to any other therapist. Will you talk
to him about the dangers of the operation when you see him.
It's very good of you to ring on his behalf. I can give him a
past-life regression, but only if he wants one. I always talk
to my clients and gather information about their history and
if they have a problem we jointly agree the change. All the
information will be confidential between him and me. If he
doesn't want to discuss problems about the sex change
operation then I will respect his views.

He came to see me shortly afterwards wearing a dress. The effect of the hormone medication was obvious from the shape of protruding breasts beneath the dress and the sound of his feminine voice. We agreed that the session would be a past-life regression and I would call him Mary. The regression was into a past-life of a girl born to parents who desperately wanted a boy. The short life was unhappy because she was the 'wrong' sex, and the death came from the loss of blood following an axe attack by a local villager. At the end of the session I gave Mary the name of a local counselor who had personally been through a sex change operation and specialized in helping in this area.

I never did find out what happened to Mary but the pattern between the planned operation in Holland and being cut to death in the past-life must have given him something to think about.

RAPPORT

The previous extract illustrates how important it is to build rapport during an interview and to maintain it during a session. This is something that that regression therapy has in line with other psychotherapies[1]. The relationship needs to be built so that painful, embarrassing or threatening information can be disclosed. A confidential and trusting relationship is essential together with a non-judgmental approach. In cases of sensitive trauma such as sexual abuse the first sessions may require rapport building and counseling before the client is ready for regression therapy.

The following extract comes from Milton Erickson, a psychiatrist in the US whose work was instrumental in establishing modern hypnotherapy. Summarized from *The Collected Papers of Milton Erickson*[2] it provides a wonderful example of how he used rapport with a psychotic patient:

A patient in Worcester State Hospital in Massachusetts demanded he be locked in his room and spent his time anxiously and fearfully winding string around the bars of the windows in the room. He knew his enemies were going to come in and kill him, and the windows were the only opening. The thick iron bars seemed to him to be too weak, so he reinforced them with string. I went into the room and also helped him reinforce the iron bars with string. In doing so I discovered that there were cracks in the floor and suggested that those cracks ought to be stuffed with newspaper so there was no possibility of his enemies getting him that way. Then I discovered cracks around the door that should be stuffed with newspaper and gradually I got him to realize that the room was only one of a number on the ward, and to accept the attendants as part of his defense against enemies, and then the Board of Mental Health of the State of Massachusetts, and then the police system and then the governor. I then spread it to the adjoining States and finally I made the United States as part of his defense system. This enabled him to dispense with the locked door because he had so many lines of defense. I did not try and correct his psychotic idea that his enemies would kill him. I merely pointed out he had an endless line of defenders. The result was the patient was able to accept ground privileges and wander the grounds safely. He ceased his frantic endeavors and was much less of a problem.

By having a non-judgmental approach and respect for the inner world of the other person Erickson demonstrated how quickly trust was gained before transforming their problem. In this case the transformation was in slow steps within the patient's ability to understand. Traditionally when a client fails to respond to therapy they are considered 'resistant'. In regression there should be no need for resistance because whatever is brought into the session should be viewed as part of the total problem.

In a study at the University of Pennsylvania the research showed that 55 per cent of our communication is received from our body, 38 per cent from our voice, and 7 per cent from the language we use. So when someone focuses consciously on the words of a conversation, 93 per cent of the communication is done subconsciously. Mirroring is a technique to help this subconscious communication. With body mirroring, a person can keep eye contact and match the other's posture and movement. Sometimes body movements cannot be immediately matched such as hand gestures or arms that suddenly cross. However, when it is time to talk, the other person's new body posture can be mirrored without it being obvious. The voice tone, rhythm and volume can be matched together with using the phrases or words the other person uses. Rapport is about being more like the other person and getting into alignment with them.

It proves useful to understand a client's belief about what will happen after death. Some may have a materialistic view, and then past-life regression can be explained as healing the problem in the subconscious memories with creative visualization and imaginative stories that resemble a past-life. Those with a more spiritual belief can have it described as healing the source of the problem from past lives. The absolute truth is less important than the client's perception that it is coherent and logical. People that are analytical can be reminded that they don't stop a film part way through to analyze it, and the same applied to a past-life regression.

Explaining how regression can help with the presented symptoms can be done with examples of clients with similar conditions. The therapist's confidence in a beneficial outcome sets a firm foundation.

THE OBJECTIVE AND SYMPTOMS

The first interview is an opportunity to gather a client's symptoms and the objectives of the session. A common failing of many therapy students is to collect vague symptoms. 'I get angry' with further questioning may turn out to be 'Two anger outbursts a day for the last three years'. 'I get panic attacks' through further questioning may be, 'only one panic attack about two years ago'. Thus the severity of the problem can be assessed and improvement of symptoms becomes easier for the client to track with the therapist.

BOUNDARIES AND HISTORY TAKING

Boundaries between the therapist and client need to be established. In a regression session emotions may be released, and body therapy may involve some physical touch via props such as cushions and the client's consent for this is needed. When trust has been damaged from experiences of being a victim it may take weeks of building a safe relationship before any form of physical contact can be made. The other boundary that needs to be established is about any communication outside of therapy sessions. This covers contact about post-therapy progress, and contact from a client who may want to talk about new problems between sessions.

An important part of history taking includes finding out what was happening in the client's life shortly before the symptoms first appeared. It also includes checking for mental health problems, physical illness and any impairment such as deafness and high blood pressure. This information enables a client's complex to be understood and those not suitable for using regression therapy identified.

COMPLEXES TO AVOID WITH REGRESSION THERAPY

Those therapists new to regression work will find the clients that they attract tend to be those that do not need a lot of work, or ones who have done a lot before with others. As more experience is gained, the ability to deal with more difficult problems will increase. Many complexes such as Obsessive Compulsion Disorder require experience of working with serious mental health problems and the integration of other psychotherapeutic approaches.

However, some client problems are areas to avoid using regression therapy. This includes clients who are unable to think clearly and rationally, or who are delusional. This includes anorexia when body weights drops below a critical weight. Lack of food protein means they are unable to produce hormones for normal brain activity. Also included is depression when it reaches an advanced stage. The symptoms of this are reduced activity levels, excessive sleeping, constant fatigue, inability to concentrate and inability to be able to work. Another contra indicator is Bipolar Disorder that alternates from major depression to manic periods of racing thoughts, easy distractibility and reduced need for sleep.

Care needs to be taken with clients with schizophrenic tendencies. They may attempt to over identify with past-life fragments and elaborate them rather than integrate them into their own psyche.

Recreational drugs or high levels of medication, particularly high levels of 'anti-depressants', and 'anti-anxiety' drugs can be contra indicators. Dose levels of these above 50mg often make concentration and memory retention difficult. The person's ability to link to their higher self is affected, making past-life memory recall and spirit realm work difficult.

Other areas to be avoided if cathartic work is used are medical conditions including heart problems or epileptic fits were experiencing higher emotional levels is not recommended. Women who are pregnant should not be regressed, because the fetus may register the emotional experiences as its own.

If the therapist is working with a child under 16 the parents written consent will be required.

THE ADVERSE EFFECTS OF PSYCHIATRIC DRUGS

The use of psychotic drugs has its place to break a spiraling cycle into deeper depression or psychosis. However, they are not a long-term solution when therapy can be used. The side effect from these drugs is startling. In the widely used drug handbook for doctors, *Psychotropic Drugs Fast Facts*, Jerrold Maxmen[3] consolidates the available research data on psychotic drugs. Some of the side effects include confusion, disorientation hallucinations, hypomania and even an *increase* in the level of anxiety and depression that they are meant to reduce.

When a client stops taking psychotic drugs there are often unpleasant side effects. The original symptoms of anxiety and depression may intensify for a short period of time. For this reason medical practitioners normally advise the pharmacy 10 per cent withdrawal method[4]. The drug is reduced in 10 steps of approximately 10 per cent at a time, with the last step sometimes divided into smaller steps. The duration of each step will vary depending upon the previous level of medication and how long it was taken. Each step is taken when in the client's judgment the withdrawal side effects from the previous step have reduced. Whilst this reduces the side-effect symptoms, a therapist needs to be aware that during the period of withdrawal the original symptoms of depression or anxiety may be troublesome.

Obviously the decision of the client to change medication levels needs to be discussed and agreed with their medical practitioner.

FALSE MEMORIES

This extract shows how easy it is to be accused of introducing a false memory:

> In September 2003 a leading child psychiatrist was accused of planting false memories of sexual abuse into the mind of a 13-year-old girl. The General Medical Council of the UK reviewed the charge against him of professional misconduct. The girl had been referred to the psychiatrist after she had stopped eating at boarding school and had taken an overdose of anti-depressant drugs. Prior to this she had been seeing a bone specialist because her parents had become concerned she was not growing fast enough for her age. During one of these sessions the bone specialist had carried out a visual examination of her breasts. The child psychiatrist claimed the girl told him the specialist had stroked her breasts. However, it was later discovered that the girl's parents had been present at all the appointments and had witnessed no such thing.

In some countries, particularly the United States, false memories allegations have resulted in therapists being sued. Although this is difficult to prove a therapist needs to take protective steps. If any form of body therapy is used in the regression process some client physical contact may take place. So as a protection against allegations of unprofessional conduct the therapist is advised to record every session. With the advent of cheap digital recorders that can record many hours continuously, the technology exists to conveniently record every session. These recordings are hiss-free so that even quietly spoken parts can be accurately recorded. The therapist also needs to be careful to ask questions rather than use leading statements, particularly if abuse information comes up during a regression session.

SUMMARY

The interview is an opportunity to decide if it is appropriate to use regression therapy or spiritual regression. Contra indications include clients who are unable to think clearly and rationally, or are delusional. This may be caused by their complex or be drug induced from recreational and medical drugs. The medical and mental health history needs to be carefully checked, and protection against allegations of false memories or unprofessional conduct is by recording every session. Building rapport starts at the interview and needs to be maintained during the sessions. This includes discussing and agreeing what will happen in the therapy and the boundaries between sessions. A confidential and trusting relationship is essential, together with a non-judgmental approach.

11

CONCLUSION

There are no mistakes, no coincidences,
all events are blessings given to us to learn from.
Elizabeth Kubler-Ross.

Growing objective evidence has been amassed through the work of Ian Stevenson and his colleagues with children's past-life accounts, and with near death experiences that are difficult to explain away except through the reality of past lives. Western science does not have an explanation so the Ancient Wisdom and its principals of soul growth through reincarnation and karma provide that theory. I have illustrated how this has been confirmed through the extensive research of Michael Newton and my own case studies of between lives soul memories. Sometimes only fragments of what appears to be a past-life may occur. A good example of this is the case study of Rose who was abused by her father. She regressed into a past-life of a soldier in a battlefield who was trapped by falling rubble from a building. As she remembered the pressure on her legs it enabled the healing to start while avoiding having to face a painful childhood memory. Her psyche was given full permission to follow its own resonance and associations first into a past-life and then into her current-life. She was able to come to a place of resolution that led to a remission of her symptoms. Searching for the truth of the past-life in this kind of therapy is not as important as its power to heal.

It may appear that regression therapy makes extravagant claims to be the therapy of therapies that rarely fails were others fail. Also, that it integrates all the key therapeutic disciples of psychotherapy and transpersonal experiences into one complete process. These claims would be exaggerated and wrong because it does not work for all people. For some clients regression therapy is too intensive and overwhelming. They may not need raw areas of their psyche exposed and simply want a therapeutic relationship that helps them rebuild their trust and confidence in life. Some may find it difficult to work with images and allow their intuition freedom to open up to past lives. Others may be so deeply stuck in a complex that they are not ready to relinquish it, and the physical and emotional pain has to be experienced for the benefit of their higher self. Reoccurring pain and disharmony is a major teacher for the soul, which is not understood by the medical profession.

Regression therapy can bring remarkable releases of chronic physical symptoms and crippling emotional conditions. Many of these have been described in the case studies. Research with regression therapy shows that 60 per cent of clients experience some level of benefit, often when other therapies have been unsuccessful. Whatever a client's belief, past-life regression allows a person to understand the patterns from this life and how they were created. Going beyond a past-life death into the spirit realms can have a profound effect, and finding forgiveness with a past-life character provides a metaphor for change in conscious thinking. Intuitive communication with spirit guides brings levels of spiritual wisdom beyond conventional therapy, and therapists are advised to take a humble role as part of a team in the healing process. I always start all regression sessions by making my intent clear for any of these spirits of light to assist me for the benefit of the client.

An important part of this therapy is recognizing that soul healing is about working with energies. A client wanted to know what had happened to him in the six hours between taking a massive drug overdose and waking in hospital after a suicide attempt. The doctors had been at a loss to explain how he had survived a drug level six times higher than the normal level to cause death. When he regressed into the experience he wept at the compassion and love he had felt as his spirit guide poured energy healing into his body. It was done at a cellular level to block the effect of the drugs and then the guide explained why he had not been allowed to die. The real value in the spirit realms is the rich variety of approaches that can be used to release and transform frozen energy patterns stuck in unexpressed emotions such as fear, guilt and anger and the old recurring thoughts. It also helps therapists to identify and release the attached soul energy from other past-life characters, such as the troops who were led to their death or the slaves cruelly beaten to death.

Intrusive energy also illustrates the importance as viewing healing as working with energies rather than the traditional views of psychotherapy. Although this is controversial and difficult to prove, it appears that earthbound subtle body energies and negative energy can become attached to clients. As illustrated with the case study of Joe who had voices in his head and the research of Ron Van der Maeson in Appendix 1, quite remarkable transformations can take place by recognizing that some client's symptoms are energy attachments. William Baldwin referred to this as Spirit Releasement, and Shamans call it working with lost soul parts. The names are less important than the need for energy release and completion.

Many therapeutic approaches such as cognitive behavioral therapy are talking therapies and avoid any form of cathartic release. However, by only focusing on cognitive memories they ignore the limbic system of the brain where body and trauma core memories are stored. As early as the 1920s, Wilhelm Reich had explored the issue of rigid character structures and how they were expressed in the body. What he showed us was that these rigid structures of body armor were not the result of physical stress but a direct expression of deeply repressed emotions. Bessel van der Kolk and his researchers have found that clients need to be regressed to their frozen body energy memories so they can be activated, released and transformed before working with other memories. Alice Bailey outlined the principles governing the karmic inheritance from past lives of severe illnesses and body memories. This has been independently verified by the research of Ian Stevenson with children's physical symptoms related to violent past-life deaths. The implications of this are that for effective remembering and release of traumatic residues the body must be involved.

Spiritual regression gives detailed recall of the soul memories between lives. These memories include meeting the other members of soul groups some of whom are recognized as people from the current-life. Often a client will have had a karmic conflict with them at an earlier time in their current-life. Finding out it was pre-planned by their soul before they reincarnated is transformational in dealing with relationships. Understanding why our body and life circumstances have been selected gives further deep insights. One of the highlights of any spiritual regression is meeting the elders that through love and compassion guide the planning for the current-life. Often they give spiritual direction at a mid point in a person's life. In the history of mankind this has only been available following the completion of a life. Those spirits of light who are guiding the destiny of Earth seem to have made a decision to change the rules and accelerate soul healing through making this information more readily available. The words of Clare after her spiritual regression sum it up well:

I realize that this work has touched me on an even deeper level than I had realized. I use the word trust a lot. I now realize that I not only trust, I know that everything is perfect. It is this sense of knowing that has opened my heart and my soul. I feel re-connected, I know where I am, I know why I came, I know that the choices I make are perfect at the time I make them and I know that I am loved.

Buddha indicated the steps for soul healing, which are timeless aspects of the Ancient Wisdom. The first step is recognizing a problem exists at a conscious level. The second step is to know what caused it. Past-life and spiritual regression help people to see beyond the personality-contained illusion and confusion of this life. The third step is to know what to do. Regression therapy unfreezes the emotional and physical charges that can make change so difficult, and the transcendent spiritual experiences give new insights. The fourth step is to change the way we think and our actions towards others in our present life. Integration after a past-life and spiritual regression helps, but in end it is up to the client to make the change and use their free will to spiritually grow and develop.

Why these powerful tools to help soul healing should be made available at this moment of time is not clear but is probably connected to the difficult juncture in humanity's history. With all the mistakes being made due to greed and materialism, so much in the world can be changed by our awareness of the duality that exists, the power of positive intention and respect for karma. In the words of the Ancient Wisdom, 'We came from love and we return to love.'

APPENDIX I - NOTES

1 – THE HISTORY OF REGRESSION THERAPY

Working with past lives started around 30 years ago with the teacher and author Dr Morris Netherton. Dr Hans TenDam the author of *Deep Healing*, built on this work and introduced new techniques. He was responsible for training most of the regression therapists in Holland and approximately one third of those in Brazil. Dr Roger Woolger over a 20-year period has integrated psychodrama, Reichian body awareness, Jung's theory of complexes into his own version of regression therapy that he calls Deep Memory Processes (DMP). Regression therapy has been taken into the traditional medical world. This includes the work of Professor Mario Simoes in the Facility of Medicine in Portugal and Terumi Okuyama M.D. the first medical doctor in Japan to integrate past-life regression as part of medical treatment in Japan. Other pioneers are Dr Pavel Gyngazov a medical doctor who has used regression therapy in Russia, Dr Newton Kondavati M.D. in India and Julio Peres M.D. in Brazil. Others that have brought new awareness of past lives includes Professor Ian Stevenson research with children's spontaneous past lives, and Dr Michael Newton who has spent 30 years methodically recording client's soul memories between lives using deep hypnosis.

This is in no way meant to exclude the efforts of many others worldwide, but to indicate the many different ways that some of the pioneers have contributed.

2 - RESEARCH WITH REGRESSION THERAPY

Dr Ron Van der Maesen's groundbreaking research using regression therapy has been with clients who had conditions commonly thought untreatable with psychotherapy. His first research study was with Tourettes's syndrome[1]. This is a disorder characterized by involuntary repetitive behaviors, and has been considered as a lifelong neuro-psychiatric condition. His research was conducted using ten members of the Dutch Association of Regression Therapy, with 22 subjects over the age range of nine to fifty-two years old. All of the subjects were under medical care and taking medication to control their tics. Of the ten subjects who completed the therapy and responded to a one-year follow-up questionnaire, five reported that their motor tics had for the most part largely disappeared or been greatly reduced in frequency. The same applied to vocal tics. Five subjects also reported that they were free of medication.

His second research study[2] was with clients who had disturbing voices or thoughts, many of whom met the diagnosis of auditory hallucinations of schizophrenia as defined in *Diagnostic and Statistical Manual of Mental Disorders* (*DSM-IV*). He worked with 54 subjects split into a therapy and a control group. The Dutch Association of Regression Therapy supplied the therapists for the research. At a six-month follow-up after the therapy by an external psychiatrist 25 per cent reported that the voices had disappeared, and a further 32 per cent could now cope with the voices. Over all, 80 per cent had a positive subjective experience and would recommend this therapy for these problems in others. In his critical review of psychotherapy in the book *What Works for Whom*[3], Professor Fonagy points out that other psychological treatments for schizophrenia appear not to be effective for as many as half those suffering from this disorder. In the other half, improvements have only been noted in the area of delusions.

In a large scale practice based research study Helen Wambach[4] reported on the results of a survey of 26 past-life regression therapists who had worked with a total of 17,350 clients with past-life regression. Of these, 63 per cent improved their emotional and physical symptoms, and 40 per cent improved their interpersonal relationships. One significant aspect about this study was that many of the clients had only turned to this therapy when other therapeutic approaches had been unsuccessful.

Hazel Denning[5] conducted large-scale, practice-based research using eight past-life regression therapists with nearly 1,000 clients between 1985 and 1992. The results were measured just after the therapy, after six months, after one year, and after five years. Of the 450 clients who could still be tracked after five years, 24 per cent reported the symptoms had completely gone, 23 per cent reported a considerable or dramatic improvement, 17 per cent reported a noticeable improvement and 36 per cent reported no improvement.

3 - VISUALIZATION USED IN PSYCHOTHERAPY

Guided imagery has a long and respectable history in psychotherapy. As early as 1935 Jung[6] proposed the use of 'active imagination' as the cornerstone of his method and by the 1940s Roberto Assagioli[7] had made guided imagery meditations the foundation for his therapy he called Psychosynthesis. Deep respect for the power of imagination in psychotherapy also forms the basis of Transpersonal Psychotherapy[8]. Milton Erickson who was one of the significant figures in developing modern-day hypnotherapy also pioneered the used of metaphors and stories as powerful healing techniques[9]. The work of Erickson was also the foundation of the widely used therapy called NLP[10]. Another example of guided imagery is in the therapy called Metaphor Therapy developed by David Groves[11]. The very core of this therapy involves the therapist working interactively with the client in developing an image or a metaphor of the client's problem. It is not an exaggeration to say that practically all psychotherapy and hypnotherapy procedures entail some level of imagery.

4 - CATHARSIS

Sigmund Freud first used the term catharsis after he discovered the symptoms of his client Anna O. disappeared after she had expressed previous suppressed emotions. He later abandoned the use of catharsis when he discovered that her symptoms had reappeared some years after the completion of therapy. Others continued to work with catharsis including one of the founders of body awareness Reich and later by Moreno. What Freud missed and Moreno realized was that catharsis is more than releasing an emotional charge of suppressed rage, fear, anger, and sadness. Moreno saw it as an opportunity for the client to gain new insights and to transform them into their present life. These ideas were included into his group therapy that was successfully used in clinical outpatient groups and the mental health organizations in the United States. Some of the widely know psychotherapies using the release of trapped energy and integration include Fritz Perl's Gestalt Therapy, Psychodrama[12], Rebirthing and Inner Child Therapy. These therapies show that very strong or inadequately expressed emotions associated with an image may make it impossible for that perception to change without the emotion being first released. When it has been released the client can be helped to see it in a different light and have a more accurate perception[13]. Dr Hans TenDam, Dr Roger Woolger and many other regression therapists have found that repressed and blocked emotions need to released and transformed to heal deep complexes.

Hypnotherapy and many psychotherapy techniques, including the widely used Cognitive Behavioral Therapy take a different view and call a catharsis an 'abreaction' and try to avoid it. Past-life therapists using hypnosis are taught desensitization. The idea is to briefly uncover the situation or regressed negative memory and allow the conscious mind to digest it slowly as a detached observer. The focus is to bring the past-life to conscious awareness rather than release and transform the complex.

5 - BODY MEMORIES

The importance of physical release as well as its accompanying emotional release has been underlined by the trauma therapy developed by Bessel Van der Kolk[14]. The Harvard psychiatric researchers he worked with emphasize the involvement of older parts of the brain structure, particularly the reptilian or limbic system. This part of the brain responds to life-or-death issues of survival and is responsible for storing traumatic emotional and body memories. The lower portions of the limbic area control sensation and movement, and the intermediate parts control emotional processing[15]. This part of the brain is separate from the frontal cortical of the brain normally used for logic and thinking. The implications of this are that for effective remembering and the release of traumatic residues the body must be involved.

The Ancient Wisdom[16] explains how physical memories are held as an etheric memory in the subtle body. A girl in a past-life who is strangled to death will have the physical sensations of choking for air at the point of dying. This becomes an etheric memory retained in the subtle body as it departs from the physical body. This memory can then be imprinted in a later lifetime in the malleable body of the baby when the soul merges with it. In line with the more physical releases sought by Wilhelm Reich, working with past-life body memories very frequently brings about a spontaneous dissolving of body armor and the recovery of blocked physical libido. Indeed, a striking aspect of much of this approach when seen by an observer for the first time is the obvious physical involvement of the client in the story that is being relived. As Roger Woolger[17] has found, a client with a chronic physical holding pattern doesn't just sit or lie passively recounting an inner vision with his or her eyes closed. Instead they may be subject to dramatic body movements such as clutching their stomach in reliving a spear wound, or crouched as they relive a beating as a slave. This is a fundamental difference from a past-life regression that uses hypnosis and aims only for a cognitive and spiritual understanding and neglects the body. By contrast working with body memories focuses the client on their body for the simple reason that it is in the body that physical memories are more vividly remembered.

APPENDIX II

STRUCTURING A REGRESSION THERAPY SESSION

PREPARATION

Have a recorder ready for the therapist's protection against introducing false memories, or if a client asks for a past-life recording.

A comfortable support is needed for the client to lie on that allows for body movement in regression therapy. A reclining chair with head support can be used if hypnosis is being used.

Have a room free from disruptive noises, with telephones and mobiles switched off, including the client's mobile.

A box of tissues is handy for any emotional release.

INTERVIEW

The purpose of this is for the therapist to decide if working with the client with regression is applicable. It is also to establish rapport, win trust and soften any client anxiety.

Collect the client history. In the initial interview the client's personal details, history and current problem needs to be gathered and checked for contra indications. Check if the client is on medication or has seen mental health professionals or therapists.

Agree the client objectives. The change the client wants from therapy will need to be discussed and realistic expectations of timescales established. Another client's case study can be used to illustrate the regression therapy process:

What has brought you to see me today?
Which of your problems is the most important for us to start working with first? (For a long list of problems)
After we start therapy what will be the first thing you will notice that will let you know that you are improving?

Gather the client symptoms. Measurable thought, emotional and physical symptoms enable the improvement to be tracked during therapy, such as panic attacks lasting 30 minutes, twice a week for two years:

When you last had this problem what emotions did you have?
How frequently do you experience these emotions? Daily, weekly, monthly?
What aspect of your social or working life does this emotion disrupt?
How long does the emotional condition last?
When you get these emotions what thoughts do you have with them?
What body tensions or pain do you have with them?

Therapy timescale. Every session will be different to some degree from every other regression, but some features and stages are common. Regression therapy sessions are typically planned for two hours duration. The interview section typically takes 20 minutes, 80 minutes to bridge and process the regression, 20 minutes for integration. Many therapists find it useful to do an initial interview before starting sessions.

Avoid friends sitting in. The information that comes from the session is very personal, and friends or spouses may be part of the karmic information. For this reason it is best that they do not sit in at the session. The client can always share the information later if they wish.

Address any client concerns. The therapist can explain what will happen in the session. Unsettled clients can be encouraged to have an open mind. Analytical clients can be reminded that they don't stop a film part way through to analyze it, and the same applied to a past-life or spiritual regression.

Get consent for intense sessions. Body therapy involves physical movement and some client contact may be made via props. The release of regressed or frozen memories may involve the release of intense emotions. This needs to be discussed and agreed.

REGRESSION BRIDGES

Linking to past lives can use hypnosis and guided imagery. Regression therapy bridges come from the information gathered about the client's problem. For thoughts use a key phrase from the interview until an emotion emerges:

Take a deep breath and repeat the words several times and see what happens.
Put all you focus on the emotion and go deeply into it, deep to the very core.
Go back to when you first experienced this emotion ... now what's happening?

For emotions symptoms when a current-life memory linked to it is being recalled:

What was the worst part?
Put all you focus on the emotion and go deeply into it, deep to the very core.
Go back to when you first experienced this emotion ... what's happening?

For unexplainable physical symptoms:

What sensations are you experiencing in your body? Is it near the surface or deep ... over a wide area or small area?
Adjust your body posture, arm and the leg position that goes with this memory. See if the sensations intensify.
It's as if ... what is happening?
What images are coming up

An energy scan can be used to amplify body sensations or emotions:

I'm going to scan your energy field to look for a blockage you have related to (the problem)

Scan the body 2 or three times naming the body part being scanned:

With your eyes closed focus on the area around your body as my hand moves slowly several inches from your body from your toes to your head. Tell me when you are aware of a blockage, or a lightness or heaviness ... tension ... or some other body

sensation ... or you may be aware of an emotion. Starting with the energy around your feet ... lower legs ... knees ... (and so on)
Which is the strongest sensation. Just focus on that area.
Put your whole conscious awareness in that area.

Then use the physical bridge.

EMBODY THE PAST-LIFE CHARACTER

Gather detailed information about the past-life character and ensure the experience is reported in the present tense and from within the body. If the client enters directly into a spontaneous catharsis this information can be gathered later:

What have you got on your feet, are they bare or do you have shoes on?
Describe the clothes you are wearing on your body.
What does the material feel like against your skin?
Are you carrying anything?
Are you a man or woman ... young or old?

ESTABLISH THE SCENE

Build up information about the past-life scene. Other questions that can be asked are based on how the past-life story emerges:

Are you in the country or near some buildings?
Describe it in detail.
Are you alone or with someone?
What are the other people doing?

What clothes are they wearing?
What else are you aware of around you?
Is it daytime or night-time?

EXPLORE THE PAST-LIFE

Use direct commands to move the client forwards through the past-life to the death point. Skip mundane details and go for the significant parts of the past-life. Look for shutdown points or turning points:

What happens next?
Is there any thing else of significance before we move on?
When I've counted to three go to the next significant event ... 1 ... 2 ... 3 ... now what's happening?
When I've counted to three go back to the first significant event ... 1 ... 2 ... 3 ... now what's happening?

CATHARSIS

For a spontaneous catharsis allow the release. Use sensory wording in a louder than normal voice and repeat them.

Let it all come out ... go through it body.
Body, go to the end.

THE DEATH TRANSITION

The death point always needs to be covered. Unfinished thoughts and feelings at the point of death are deeply imprinted and need to be recorded for later clearing. Physical memories can be noted from the drama such as difficulty breathing or clutching a wound:

> **When I count to three go to the moment just before your heart stops beating for the last time … 1 … 2 … 3 …now what's happening?**
> **What thoughts and emotions do you leave the life with?**

For a violent death go through the death quickly to minimize any discomfort. This needs to be said with a raised voice and the latter part repeated:

> **Go quickly to the death point … It's all over now.**

Ensure that spirit leaves the body and is not earthbound. If not find a way of ensuring that it leaves for the spirit realms:

> **Do you stay with the body or do you leave it?**
> **What is needed for you to finally leave the body?**

CONFRONTING THE OTHERS IN THE SPIRIT REALMS

New insights come from meeting the past-life characters and spirit guides can be introduced to help. True forgiveness is profoundly healing and often indicates completion:

> **Go to the place where** (the other past-life character) **is and meet them. What do you want to say to them that you could never say in that life?**
> **What do they say to you?**
> **Telepathically show your hurt to them. What happens now?**

Send a small fragment of love energy to them. What happens now?
Can you let them go now?
Ask your spirit guides to join you. What advise do they offer?

Body Therapy - Exploring Body Memories

This can be used for current-life or past-life memories and often releases a catharsis. A firm and directive voice is required:

Go to the point just before ... (i.e. you first felt the beating)
Body show me what is happening. (Encourage arm and leg movement)
Body show me what happens next. (Repeat as necessary)
Body go to the end. (This will need repeating loudly during a catharsis)

Body Therapy - Transform the Body Memory

This is best done immediately after exploring the body memories, in which case time needs to be allowed for body to relax after any catharsis. Extra energy will be needed to transform a shutdown and can come from a spirit animal:

Body (fist etc) **what do you want to do that you could never do?**
Go to the animal kingdom and find a spirit animal that has the energy you need. Bring the animal energy inside

you and feel the strength of the energy going inside (the body parts for transformation)

Review what you will be going to do for the transformation.

Go to the point just before ... (i.e. you first felt the beating)

Transform the body story using props i.e. cushions, twisted towels etc. Build the tension before allowing the transformation or provide some resistance during the transformation.

Body (or fist etc) **show me what you always wanted to do.**

CURRENT-LIFE REGRESSION

Current-life memories can be seen as an extension of the significant events from a past-life. They may come from the client interview or a bridge can be used from the past-life:

Go to the point in your current-life when you felt the anger (or fear etc) **and tell me what is happening.**

Once the current-life memories have been reviewed they can be transformed in a similar way to past-life memories by dialogue with the characters from these events:

Allow yourself to connect with (the person). **What do you want to say that you could never say at the time?**

What do they say to you?

Completion

An energy scan can pick up a residual energy blockage. If any is found then a regression back to that point will be needed and spirit realm or body therapy transformation can be used.

Integration

Questions at the end of a past-life session start the process of integration:

Do you recognize any patterns from that life being worked out in this life?
Do you recognize any of the people from that past-life working out in this life?

For a single therapy session a feedback phone call or email can assist the integration. In multiple sessions a journal of past lives can be kept by the client, physical activities encouraged for dissociation, and the past-life can be reviewed before the start of a new session.

The Exit Interview

The client needs to sit up for this part of the session and still be in a state of reflection. The therapist's task is to assist the client so they can find their own interpretation of the session. A period of at least 10 minutes should be set aside talking to the client and ensuring they are fully grounded.

Appendix III

Structuring a Spiritual Regression Session

The methodology in this section including the scripts and questions are adapted from Dr Michael Newton's book, *Life Between Lives Hypnotherapy*,[1] and used in the Training Manual of the Michael Newton Institute.

Preparation

The aim is to make every spiritual regression successful.

Screen the client. Check they have successfully experienced hypnosis and a past-life before a spiritual regression. Those that haven't can be asked to have a separate past-life regression using hypnosis. Clients will go into deeper levels when they have experienced trance or similar altered states of awareness previously. Providing a self-hypnosis CD may help in this. Contra indicators can be checked particularly medication, recreational drugs or emotional upheavals. The spiritual regression is not intended to release and clear trauma.

Have a recorder ready. The session needs to be recorded because the client will not remember all the details of the spiritual regression. Clients often play the recording a number of times to get new insights. It is also useful to use a second recording system as backup.

The client's body needs comfortable support. The sessions are between three and four hours in duration. In deep trance the client will not be able to change their physical position to relieve any pressure so it is important for them to be comfortable. A therapist couch, sofa or reclining chair can be used. A blanket will help ensure they don't get cold when their circulation slows.

Have a room free from disruptive noises. Telephones and mobiles need to be switched off, including the client's mobile.

The length of the session needs planning. This can be up to four hours so ample time needs set aside by the client for the session and for a stress free period afterwards to reflect on the experience. These regressions are energy intensive for the therapist because for most of the period they will be intuitively linked with the spiritual helpers. To avoid 'therapist burn out' it is recommended a maximum of one spiritual regression in a day should be planned.

Create a sacred space for the session. The therapist's primary resource is their intuitive link. If they are not using their normal setting they need to be comfortable with the surroundings and its energy space. A CD player can be used for celestial background music and assist in the hypnosis process.

Pre-work for the client before the session. A suggested verbal or email instruction to the client is:

'Thank you for your enquiry. Before having a spiritual between lives regression it is important that you have had hypnosis successfully. This is because deep hypnosis is required to access your soul memories. Trance is a natural state of consciousness during which the mind becomes inwardly focused and analytical thinking drifts into the background. Light trance happens every day quite naturally. An example is driving a car for an extended period when we remember little of the journey except for our inner thoughts.

Going into deep trance is a collaborative effort. People who are already familiar with trance tend to enter into the hypnotic state more rapidly and with greater depth than those encountering this altered state of consciousness for the first time.

If you haven't had hypnosis you could find someone locally or if you send me your address I can supply a self-hypnosis tape for relaxation. The more times people use hypnosis the deeper level they can access.

It's also important that a past-life has been experienced before the date of the spiritual regression. A past-life regression normally lasts for 2 hours and costs *** and will be held at ***. Possible dates and times are ****.

The spiritual regression session lasts up to four hours and costs *** and will be held at ***. Possible dates and times are ***.

I will provide a CD recording of the session but you can bring your own digital recorder if you wish. Clients have found that to fully absorb the information, they often listen to the recoding a number of times. I need you to think about your objectives for the session. Possible ones include your current-life purpose, spiritual and karmic progress, why certain events have happened in your life, spotting soul group members in this life and meeting your spirit guide. Also identify up to eight significant people in your life who have had either positive or negative impact on you. State the relationship they have with you and list three adjectives for each, for example, Joanne – Mum: loving, controlling, remote.

Because of the length of the session it would be good for you to wear comfortable clothing and to lie down during the session. It is not recommended that friends sit in on the session because much of the information maybe personal.

You can always share the information on your recording at a later date.

It is also recommend that you plan a leisurely time immediately after the session and allow plenty of time for your return journey if you need to drive a car.'

BEGINNING OF THE SESSION

The purpose of this is for the therapist to establish rapport, win trust, provide encouragement and soften any client anxiety.

Collect the client's details. The client's personal details need to be collected and checked for past-life regression contra indicators. The client's age will need to be collected and if they are aware of childhood trauma or are unable to remember periods of their childhood this is an indicator to either avoid or be careful using the age-regression deepener. Client's that have experienced hypnosis before can be asked about the techniques that were most effective and some of these can be substituted into the hypnosis induction or deepening. Analytical clients may need a confusion induction.

Address any client concerns. The therapist can explain what will happen in the session and address any concerns. Clients can be reminded that they will be able to indicate the need to go to the toilet even in the deepest of hypnosis.

Set expectations of what will happen. A client's experiences may be different from what they may have read on the subject. Some sessions are in great detail and some less so, some with visual experiences and some without. The client can be advised to be open to the universe and allow the experience to come to them in whatever form is appropriate.

Review the client's preparation. The objectives and lists of significant people can be reviewed.

Avoid friends sitting in. The information that comes from the session is very personal and friends or spouses may be part of the karmic information. For this reason its best that they do not sit in at the session. The client can always share the information on the session recording later if they wish.

HYPNOSIS - TRANCE INDUCTION

Up to 45 minutes of trance induction and deepening may be needed to take a client to the deep levels where they have free access to the detailed information of their soul memories. The therapist's voice needs to provide a rhythm using pauses, and it is helpful to gradually slow down the rate of speaking during the process of induction. Gentle celestial background music can be used to mask any irritating background noise. Ensure that the client is relaxed and lying down or fully supported in a reclining chair. His or her hands need to be visible to the therapist. The flow of suggestions can to be synchronized when possible with the client breathing out:

'As you let your eyes close ... take several deep breaths ... and focus on your breathing ... and as you breathe in ...breathe in relaxation ... and as you breathe out ... breathe out any tension ... and now focus of the top of your head ... and let any muscle tension go ... just relax and let go ... and I wonder if the deep relaxation and restful heaviness in your forehead ... is already beginning to spread ... down across your eyes ... your face ... into your mouth ... and jaw ... through your neck ... deep restful ... heavy ... and the more you physically relax ... the more you can mentally relax too ... and very soon ... you can enjoy that pleasant feeling ... of total relaxation ... and I wonder how quickly the relaxation will spread ... to your neck and shoulder muscles

... and on to the tops of your arms ... allowing those muscles to sag and become tension free .... and on to the lower arms ... feeling them relax ... down to your elbows ... and on to your forearms ... just letting all those muscles relax ... and letting go ... down to the wrists ... the hands and fingers and thumbs ... right to the tips of your fingers ... just let all the muscle tension go ... and notice your breathing becoming easier and even ... perhaps beginning to notice the sounds which were distracting becoming less so ... that all the sounds you can hear become part of your experience of comfort and relaxation ... and anything else you can notice becomes part of this experience ... and now I want you to use your wonderful imagination ... and image that you are visiting a beautiful old country house ... a really beautiful ... old country house ... on a warm ... sunny summer afternoon ... and you are standing on a staircase ... that leads down to an entrance door ... and as you look down ... you can just glimpse through the open door .... an enchanting country garden ... and its so inviting to go down the stairs ... .to discover this special place ... it's a beautiful sunny summer afternoon .... and there is no one around ... to trouble you ... or bother you ... and in a moment I will count down from one to ten ... and let each count represent a step ... and each step takes you deeper ... and into deeper levels of relaxation ... so that by the time I get to ten ... you can allow yourself to be as deeply relaxed ... as you ever can be ... and you will still hear the sound of my voice ... one ... when you are ready take your first step down ... relaxing ... and letting go ... two ... .take another step ... feeling more at ease.....and at peace with yourself ... three ... perhaps noticing a heavy, restful feeling spreading with every step... four ... just drifting deeper ... and deeper ... five ... another step ... becoming calmer ...

and calmer still ... continuing to relax ... continuing to let go ... and feeling good ... six ... feeling more and more the real enjoyment of this relaxation ... and comfort ... seven ... sinking deeper and deeper ... drifting further into this welcoming relaxed state ... eight ... enjoying those feelings ... half awake and half asleep ... and feeling very good ... nine ... noticing the growing relaxation ... and spreading comfort ... ten ... and now at the bottom of the stairs ... and wandering to the open door ... and the gardens beyond ... soak up the atmosphere of peace ... and tranquility ... in this lovely old building ... and wandering out through the door ... stand there and notice the beautiful green lawn ... the shrubs and trees ... the greens ... and browns ... and the clear blue sky ... and feel the warmth of the sun on your head and shoulders ... as you enjoy this beautiful summers afternoon ... in this lovely country garden ... and the flower beds with splashes of color ... red ... yellow ... purple ... white ... breathe in ... and smell the special perfume of this place ... and there is no one about ... no one wanting anything from you ... no one needing anything ... no one expecting anything ... so you can enjoy the peace ... and the tranquility ... in this lovely country garden ... and walking along the lawn ... coming to an archway with flowers ... and some stone steps ... lovely old steps ... and the enchanting sounds of running water in the distance ... and how inviting to go deeper to this hidden place ... and walk slowly down these steps ... and sink further and further into relaxation ... and at the bottom of the steps ... you see another lawn ... and in the distance a small stream ... with reeds growing at the side ... and you walk slowly across the grass ... enjoying this beautiful ... peaceful ... summers afternoon ... sit by the stream ... and as you do ... just look into the clear smooth water ... and let your mind go free ... and be aware of your total relaxation ... and allow your mind to drift ... where ever it wants.'

HYPNOSIS DEPTH ASSESSMENT

Either of the following involves physical signaling that can provide a useful test for trance depth and can be used at any point. Depth of trance can be assessed by the delay in response and slow jerky movement of the finger. Also in deeper trance the command will be interpreted literally so the finger will continue to rise until acknowledged:

'Pay attention to your left leg ... feeling heaviness ... just enough to notice ... and when you do ... raise a finger on your left hand ... good ... and become aware of a pleasant relaxed feeling throughout your whole body.'

'Imagine a scale ... with 10 representing wide-awake ... and 1 representing the deepest relaxation you can possibly go too ... and as I count down the scale from 10 to 1 .... let the finger on your hand lift to indicate your depth of trance ... 10 ... 9... 8... 7...' and so on.
Wait for a finger to lift, 'Good'

HYPNOSIS DEEPENING

The following deepener sometimes called 'dropping the numbers' can be used as an alternative to the Newton age regression deepener to get extra trance depth:

'In a moment I would like you to begin counting ... starting with the number one and counting upwards .... and with each number you count you will become more and more relaxed ... more comfortable ... and counting slowly ... counting very slowly and noticing that after a few numbers ... the numbers will just fade away ... and eventually the numbers will just disappear altogether ... just drift away completely because you will be so comfortable ....and so relaxed ... and those numbers will not matter anymore ... and starting with the number one counting upwards now'

Between the client's counted numbers any of the following can be used:

'drifting'
'even deeper'
'deeper and deeper'
'noticing the numbers beginning to fade away ... just fade away'
'deeper and deeper ... as the numbers fade away'
'wonderful deep relaxation'

The clients voice will go softer as the numbers fade away.

'Just drifting and floating in this wonderful deep relaxation ... and nothing else seems important ... just drifting away and enjoying this wonderful relaxation ... and in a moment I'm going to count from 1 to 5 ... and with each count you will become even more relaxed ... and more comfortable ... my the time I get 5 your relaxation will have doubled ... 1 ... drifting down ... 2 .... deeper and deeper ... 3 ... floating and drifting ... 4 ... so comfortably relaxed ... 5 ... completely comfortable and relaxed ... and you can really enjoy this wonderful deep relaxation ... feeling the deep ... deep comfort'

ANCHOR THE TRANCE DEPTH

The client's experience can be anchored at the deepest part of their trance to quickly take them to that level at later points if needed:

"Allow yourself to go to a special place where you felt relaxed ... it may have been a holiday or a place you know ... perhaps a beach ... or a place in nature ... perhaps near a stream or wood ... and when you have found your special place ... take in the scene around you ... what you are doing ... where you are ... and fill in the details..... what you are wearing ....and seeing ... and touching .... any sounds ... breathe in and smell this place ... and now focus on the feelings ... and I want you to really remember how it feels inside .... and anytime in this session when you hear me say the words ... STAY WITH THE EXPERIENCE ... you may allow yourself to go this special place ..... and experience this state of relaxation .... and lift a finger on your left hand if you understand .... good."

FINAL INSTRUCTIONS

These instructions need to have a more directive tone from the therapist:

'As we progress you will find you are able to talk to me freely ... about anything without awakening ... in fact the conversation we will have together will only serve to maintain your trance depth ... I want you to visualize having a powerful golden shield of light around you ... from head to toe ... giving you light and power ... and should any negative feelings of the past come through they will bounce off your protective shield of light.'

ENTERING THE PAST-LIFE

'And we are going to find a mist leading to your last past-life ... or another one that your higher mind selects for you ... knowing that you will emerge from the mist on the count of 3 into that past-life ... 1 ... stepping into the mist ... 2 ... starting to emerge from the mist ... allowing the memories to become stronger and clearer .... and on the next count you will be completely out of the mist and in your body in that past-life ... 3 ... notice the mist clearing as you look down at your feet ... and your legs ... and the clothing on your body ... and in your own time ... as the mist totally clears ... tell me about the clothes you are wearing.'

EMBODY THE CHARACTER

Gather detailed information about the past-life character and move through any spontaneous catharsis quickly. Possible questions are:

What have you got on your feet, are they bare or do you have shoes on?
Describe your clothes in detail.
What does the material feel like against your skin?
Are you carrying anything?
Are you a man or woman ... young or old?

ESTABLISH THE SCENE

Build up information about the past-life scene. Other questions can be asked based on how the past-life story emerges. Possible questions are:

Are you in the country or near some buildings?
Describe it in detail.
Are you alone or with someone?
What are the other people doing?
What clothes are they wearing?
What else are you aware of around you?
Is it daytime or night-time?
Is it hot or cold?

EXPLORE THE PAST-LIFE

Use direct commands to move the client forwards through the past-life. Skip mundane details and go for the significant parts of the past-life:

What happens next?
When I've counted to three go to the next significant event ... 1 ... 2 ... 3 ... now what's happening?

PAST-LIFE DEATH POINT

The past-life should be kept brief to approximately 15 to 30 minutes because it is normally reviewed in more detail with the spirit guide in the soul memories. Going to the death point is always significant and signals the end of the physical reincarnation. Suggestive statements and questions include:

Move to the time just before you take your last breath and tell me what is happening.

For a violent death go through the death quickly to minimize any discomfort.

Go quickly to the death point. It's all over now.

ENTRY TO THE SPIRIT REALMS

There is no need to gather great detail at this point. Allow longer for response to questions at this point. Useful questions to ask are:

Go to the point when your heart stops for the last time.
Do you stay with your body or are you ready to leave it?
After your heart has stopped for the last time what to you experience happening next?

Often there will be some confusion during the period of leaving the body so directional questions can be used. Possible one include:

Go to the point when you leave your body and tell me what happens next?
Do you leave by yourself or feel any sort of pull?
Are you looking down at the Earth, or in front of you?
As you move on do you see a single light or a number of lights in the distance?
Does any light drift closer to you or do you go to the light?
As the light gets closer describe the colors or the physical appearance you see?

THE PLACE OF ENERGY HEALING

If the past-life has been traumatic, clients will report going to a place of energy healing. Its purpose is to reduce their negative energy or add new energy before they can meet other souls in the spirit realms:

Where are you going next?
Describe the place that you have been drawn to go to?
Is this different in any way from other times you have been here?
Are you receiving any new energy or having old energy removed?
Describe what you experience?
Look at the color of your energy field and tell me the changes from when you first entered.

EXPLORE THE SOUL MEMORIES

These questions can be asked frequently:

What happens next?
Let me know if any other significant events happen here before we move on.

REVIEWS WITH THE SPIRIT GUIDE

Clients who have not seen their spirit guide before will find the experience will stay with them for the rest of their lives. This is often the time when the last past-life will be reviewed. Possible questions are:

Do you have any thoughts of who has met you?
Is your guide showing them-self in energy or physical form?

What do you experience when you meet your spirit guide?

Ask your guide to show them-selves in physical form and describe their appearance.

Describe the facial features.

Describe the hair color, length and eye color.

What is the name of your guide?

If your guide reviews your past-life, what is communicated?

Describe how you are shown the past-life?

Does your guide tell you the purpose for that past-life?

Did you achieve that purpose? What problems did you have?

Tell me about your guide's role in helping you in that life?

MEETING THE SOUL GROUP

All clients have a group of soul companions. Sometimes they move to this space right away without prompting and describe lights coming towards them:

Focus on the lights one by one and describe the colors?

Look into the core and tell me what color you notice?

Is this the same color as yours or different in any way?

What do you experience being with them again?

Count them and tell me how many are there in your soul group.

Have any of your soul group been involved with you in your past lives?

Is there a common interest or theme that your group are working with?

Focus on your soul group one by one and tell me the names of any that you recognize in your current-life.
Did you do any preparation for this life with them at this point?
How many lifetimes have you had with this group?
Do any members of your group spend extended periods away pursuing other activities?

MEETING OTHER SOUL GROUPS

If the client is part of another soul group they may describe going to other lights. Possible questions are:

Focus on the lights one by one and describe the colors?
Look into the core and tell me what color you notice?
Is this the same color as yours or different in any way?
Focus on them one by one and tell me about any that you recognize in your current-life.
Did you do any preparation for this life with them at this point?
Is there a common interest or theme that your group are working with?
How many lifetimes have you had with this group?

VISITING THE ELDERS

All souls will at some point visit the elders (or another name given) at least once between lives. This is one of the most important parts of a life between lives session and a major focus area. At some point in the client may describe leaving a place with their spirit guide. If you want to go straight to this event:

Go to the place where you meet the spirits of light who planned your incarnation for your current-life.

Establish the scene in detail. It can be in physical form or energy form. Possible questions are:

Describe your travel route. Let me know what you notice and what happens when you arrive.
Describe the place that you arrive at.
Is their any difference in the surroundings since your last visit?
Is your spirit guide with you?
Tell me the position of your spirit guide relative to you.
What are you experiencing as you visit this place?

Gather information about the elders. They may be in physical form or energy form. The possible questions are:

How many spirits of light are there?
What name do you call them?
Look closely. Are they in energy form or human form?
Describe the facial features you are aware of.
Describe the hair color, length and eye color.
Find the most prominent one and describe how they are dressed and any ornament or emblem you notice.
What is the significance of that ornament or emblem to you?

Find out what is communicated with the elders. The possible questions are:

What is communicated to you?
What do they say to you that your Guide did not cover?

Do they offer you any encouragement or advise?
Do they review your next life and offer any advise?
Do you discuss the level of soul energy to take with you into the next life?

SELECTING THE CURRENT-LIFE PHYSICAL BODY

This is the place where the client can try out the body for their current-life and sometimes have a choice in its selection. The aim is to allow the client a greater understanding about themselves and their origin. Often it happens during the meeting with the spirit guide or elders. To go straight to this event:

Go to the place where you select your body for this life.

Other possible questions to ask in the place of body selection are:

Describe the surroundings?
Is your guide with you or are you by yourself?
How many body choices do you have?
How are the bodies being shown to you?
What do you think each body offers you?
Do you have a choice life or family or circumstances with each body?
Why do you reject some choices?
How will the body you select help you achieve your life purpose?
Do you have choice of emotions or intelligence with the body selected?
Do you have any discussions about how much of your soul energy will you be taking with you?

OTHER SPIRITUAL ACTIVITIES

The following list includes some of the things the client may experience at some point in the soul memories. Many questions can be asked intuitively as a result of the answer to your questions.

Possible questions when in the halls of learning or in teaching rooms:

Describe your surroundings?
What are you learning?
How does the process of learning happen?
How will this help you in your current-life?

Possible questions when in areas of solitude for study and reflection:

Describe your surroundings?
Have you been to this place before?

Possible questions to ask when traveling to another dimension or learning new knowledge:

Describe your surroundings?
How will this help you in your current-life?
Have you been to similar places after other past lives?

DEPARTING THE SPIRIT REALMS FOR REINCARNATION

This completes the soul memories and often brings new insights about the current-life. If you want to go straight to this event:

Go to the place where you prepare for the next reincarnation.

Possible questions for reincarnation are:

Describe the surroundings?
Is your spirit guide with you or are you by yourself?
How much of your soul energy will you be taking with you?
What is the reason for taking that level of energy into this reincarnation?
What emotions or physical memories will you be taking from the past-life?
How will you remember the significant people you will need to meet in this new life?
Go to the point when your soul energy merges with the baby's body in the womb. Tell me what you experience?
How old is the baby from conception when your soul merges with it?
Is their any significance of joining the baby at that age?

THE ELDERS AND THE 'ETERNAL NOW'

The therapist can also switch the meeting with the elders from memory recall to the 'eternal now' and have interactive communication to answer specific questions. It's best done after experiencing all the soul memories because it will be less confusing when the client listens to the tape afterwards:

Go back to the meeting with the elders. (or other name used).

The possible questions to ask the elders in the eternal now are:

Ask them to confirm what your purpose is for your current-life?

How many other past lives have you been working on this aspect?

Ask them to review any of these past lives that will be of help to you?

What comments do they have about your progress in this life?

Ask them to give you advice to help in your current-life?

Ask them if you can be told about your spiritual activities in the future.

Ask each elder (or other name used) **if they have any thing else to say to you?**

Is there anything else you need to ask the elders (or other name used)?

FINAL CLOSURE IN THE SPIRIT REALMS

This can be addressed to the client:

Before we leave the spirit realms I want you to tell me if there is anything we have missed of significance?

Thank all the spirits of light for their help and wisdom and release them.

AWAKENING THE CLIENT

The client will have been in deep hypnosis for up to four hours and time will be needed to allow them to come to a wide awake state, and for their blood circulation to come back to normal. In a louder than normal voice:

> 'We are now going to leave the spirit realms and you can bring back with you all the memories and insights. I'm going to count from ten to one and when we reach the count of one you will be wide awake, relaxed, fully refreshed as if awakening from a full night of sleep.
>
> Ten ... starting to come back ...
>
> Nine ... being able to move your left leg (encourage leg movement) ...
>
> Eight ... being able to move your right leg (encourage leg movement) ...
>
> Seven ... moving your left hand and arm ...
>
> Six ... moving your right hand and arm ...
>
> Five ... allowing your waist to move ...
>
> Four ... moving your shoulders ...
>
> Three ... coming back all the more ...
>
> Two ... On the next count your eyes being fully open....
>
> One ... Your eyes fully open, being fully aware of being in the room.'

THE EXIT INTERVIEW

The client needs to sit up for this part of the session and still be in a state of reflection. The therapist's task is to assist the client so they can find their own interpretation of the session. A period of at least 15 minutes should be set aside talking to the client and ensuring they are fully grounded.

Summarize the order of key events of the spiritual regression i.e. crossover, meeting soul groups etc and ask questions on the content:

What key aspects do you remember about this part and in what way was it helpful?

The client can be asked to wait for a few weeks before listening to their recording and getting further insights. After reflection they can be asked to write a summary of how the information has helped and email this to the therapist. This further helps the integration process and gives the therapist useful feedback.

FURTHER READING

The following list contains classical books that provide different perspectives on regression therapy, past lives, soul memories between lives, reincarnation, psychology and psychopathology. Further titles are contained in the bibliography.

REGRESSION THERAPY

Lucas, Winafred (ed.) *Regression Therapy: A Handbook for Professionals*. vol 1. Deep Forest Press, 1993. This comes in two volumes with articles and techniques from a wide range of regression therapists.

Ten Dam, H. *Deep Healing,* Tasso, 1996, (Order from Hans Email; tasso@damconsult.nl.) Regression therapy techniques used by Hans Ten Dam, who is one of the pioneers in regression therapy.

Woolger, R. *Healing your Past Lives*, Sounds True, 2004. Roger is one of the pioneers of introducing body awareness into regression therapy. Written primary for the general reader Roger introduces his way of using regression therapy that he calls Deep Memory Process.

PAST LIVES

Bowman, C. *Children's Past Lives*, Element, 1998. An easy to read book about Carol's personal experiences with children's past lives.

Lawton, I. *The Book of the Soul*, Rational Spiritual Press, 2004. (order from Ian website; http://www.rspress.org) This contains a summary of all the modern research supporting reincarnation and the existence of the soul.

Stevenson, I. *Twenty Cases of Suggested Reincarnation*, University, 1995. Ian worked with over 2600 children's past lives. This book shares his finding with 20 of these. It's a classical book about objective research providing evidence for past lives.

Stevenson, I. *Where Reincarnation and Biology Intersect*, Praeger Publishers, 1997. This is another book by Ian providing evidence about the link between trauma from a past-life and physical problems in the current one.

Weiss, B. *Many Lives, Many Masters*, Platkus, 1994. An easy to read account of a clinical psychologist discovering past lives through a client.

BETWEEN LIVES SPIRITUAL REGRESSION

Lawton, I. with research assistance from Tomlinson, A. *Wisdom of Souls*, Spiritual Rational Press, 2006. (Order from Ian website; http://www.rspress.org) Ten groups of elders from the between lives share profound insights on a range of spiritual, historical and philosophical topics including: the purpose of life on earth, the future of humanity, and the true nature of time and reality.

Newton, M. *Journey of Souls*, Llewellyn, 1994. The narrative is based on the between lives accounts of twenty-nine people. This important book provides a foundation and a reference of mapping out the spirit realms.

Newton, M. *Destiny of Souls*, Llewellyn, 2000. A follow on from his first book and covers the specialist roles souls take in the spirit realms.

Tomlinson, A. *Exploring the Eternal Soul*, O Books, 2007. Further graphic detail is provided of what it feels like to die and cross over, who meets us, where we go, and what we do in the spirit realms before choosing the next body for incarnation. It builds on other pioneers work and sensitively presents 15 subject's experiences so that the reader is transported into the very heart of their soul's story.

REINCARNATION IN RELIGIOUS TRADITIONS

Page, C. *The Frontiers of Health,* 1996. Written by a medical doctor about how our health can be affected by any disharmony with our energy field and soul.

Rinpoche, S. *The Tibetan Book of Living and Dying,* Rider, 1992. The Buddhist explanation of what happens after death. It also contains useful information about counselling to the dying.

Some, P.M. *Of Water and Spirit – Ritual, Magic in the Life of an African Shaman,* Penguin, 1994. An easy to read book that introduces Shamanic approaches to healing.

PSYCHOLOGY AND PSYCHOTHERAPY

Herman, J. *Trauma and Recovery.* New York: Basic Books, 1992. A useful overview for dealing with sexual abuse.

Parks, P. *Rescuing the Inner Child,* Human Horizons Series, 2002. Techniques used for inner child therapy following childhood abuse.

Ireland-Frey, L. *Freeing the Captives,* Hampton Roads Publishing, 1999. Full of interesting case histories of releasing spirit attachments.

PSYCHOPATHOLOGY

Breggin, P. *Your Drug May Be Your Problem*, Perseus Publishing, 1999. Useful advice about the effect of anti-depressant and anti-anxiety medication and the side effects the pharmaceutical companies keep quite about.

Lemma, A. *Introduction to Psychopathology*, Sage Publications, 1996. A useful overview of psychopathology and it provides an introduction to diagnose client symptoms that are the contra indicators for regression therapy or spiritual regression.

REGRESSION THERAPY ASSOCIATIONS AND PROFESSIONAL TRAINING

International Board of Regression Therapy (IBRT)

This is an independent examining and certifying board for past-life therapists, researchers and training programs. Its mission is to set professional standards for regression therapists and organizations. The website has a list of international accredited past-life and regression therapy training organizations.
Website; http://www.ibrt.org

European Academy of Regression Therapy

This is a network of IBRT accredited regression therapy trainers and training organizations that work cooperatively together in Europe, and use common content and quality standards. The website has a list of training programs offered across Europe.
Website; http://www.earth-netwok.org

European Association of Regression Therapy (EARTh)

This is an independent association with the objective to improve and enlarge the professional application of regression therapy in Europe. It provides conferences, meetings, websites, internet forums, newsletters, professional standards and certification for training schools. Every summer it offers a series of workshops for ongoing professional development.
Website; http://www.earth-association.org

The International Association for Regression Research and Therapies (I.A.R.R.T)

This is a worldwide organization for past-life regression therapists. It encourages research in past lives and regression therapy and publishes newsletters and the journals on regression techniques.
Website; http://www.iarrt.org

International Deep Memory Association (I.D.M.A.)

Originating from the work of Roger Woolger it fosters the personal growth of its members and enables them to keep in touch with one another. It publishes regular newsletters with details of training, seminars and social events.
Website; http://www.i-dma.org

Norsk forbund for Regressjonsterapi (NFRT)

This is an organization of regression therapists dedicated to expanding the professional acceptance of regression therapy in Norway. It promotes educational and research activities and the awareness of regression therapy to the general public.
Website; http://www.regresjonsterapi.no

Nederlandsse Vereniging van Reincarnatie Therapeuten (N.V.R.T.)

This is a Dutch-based organization that connects professional past-life therapists and organizes research on the effectiveness of reincarnation therapy.
Website; http://www.reincarnatietherapie.nl

The Michael Newton Institute

Formally called the Society for Spiritual Regression this is a professional organization dedicated to furthering research and advances in the practice of life-between-lives spiritual regression based on the work of Dr Michael Newton. Website; http://www.newtoninstitute.org

Schweizerischen Vereinigung für Reinkarnationslehre und Therapie (SVR)

This is a Swiss-based past-life organization.
Website; http://www.svrt.ch

Asociación Española De Técnicas Regresivas Aplicadas (AETRA)

This is a Spanish network of past-life regression therapists.
Website; http://www.mundoregresiones.com/pagina52.asp

The Scientific and Medical Network

A worldwide forum of scientists, doctors, psychologists, engineers and similar professionals who are challenging scientific materialism as an explanation of reality.
Website http://www.scimednet.org

SOURCES AND FOOTNOTES

Although most of the professionals quoted in the book have doctorates in psychology or psychiatry, I do not consistently use the title 'Dr' throughout the book. This is not intended to be disrespectful, but to avoid laborious repetition. Some of the quotes from other authors may have been slightly reworded or summarized for clarity without changing the important content. All the client case studies are summarized as they happened, with client feedback carefully recorded. Some minor changes have been made to the transcripts to avoid repetition or improve the grammar. My questions are shown in normal typeface, and the client responses in italics for consistency.

PROLOGUE

1. Don Theo Paredes and Art Roffey offer shaman training and trips to Peru. Website; www.innervisionpc.org, Email; innervisionpc@comcast.net.
2. Ipu Makunaiman and his wisdom of the rain forest trips to the Amazon.Website; www.nativeculturalalliance.org, Email; tucuxi@bellatlantic.net.
3. Joao Teixeira de Faria called 'John of God', Website; www.johnofgod.com.

CHAPTER 1 - INTRODUCTION

1. Grof. S. *Beyond the Brain*, New York; State University, 1985.
2. Assagioli, R.M.D. *Psychosynthesis: A Manual of Principles and Techniques,* Aquarian Press1990.
3. Some, P.M. *Of Water and Spirit – Ritual, Magic in the Life of an African Shaman*, Penguin, 1994.
4. Powell, A. E. *The Astral Body*, Kessinger Publishing Co., 1998.
   Powell, A. E. *The Etheric Double*, Theosophical Press, 1989.

5. Krippner, S. and Rubin, R. *Galaxies of Life; the Human Aura in Acupuncture and Kirlian Photography*, Gordon and Beach, New York, 1974.
6. Brennan, B. *Hands of Light*, Bantam, 1988.
7. Wirth, D. P. *The Effect of Non-contact Therapeutic Touch on the Healing Rate of Full Thickness Dermal Wounds,* Journal of Subtle Energies & Energy Medicine, Vol. 1 No. 1,1990.
8. *Daily Mail*, Dec 14th 2001, page 11.
9. Van Lommel et al, *Near-death Experience in Survivors of Cardiac Arrest*; a prospective study in the Netherlands, The Lancet, 15 Dec 2001.
10. Gallup, G. *A look Beyond the Threshold of Death*, London Souvenir, 1983.
11. Stevenson, I. *Twenty Cases of Suggested Reincarnation*, University, 1995.
12. Weiss, B. *Many Lives, Many Masters*, Simon and Schuster, 1988.
13. Newton, M. *Destiny of Souls*, Llewellyn, 2000.
14. Newton, M. *Journey of Souls*, Llewellyn, 1994.
15. Haraldsson, E., *East and West Europeans and their Belief in Reincarnation and Life after Death*, in SMN *Network Review*, No 87, Spring 2005.
16. Maj, M., Sartorius, N., Okasha, A., Zohar, J., *Obsessive Compulsion Disorder*, Wiley, 2000.
17. Bowlby, J. *The Making and Breaking of Affectional Bonds*, Roultledge, 1994.
18. Stevens, R. *Understanding the Self,* The Open University, SAGE Publications, 1996.

CHAPTER 2 - PAST-LIFE AND SPIRITUAL REGRESSION THEORY

1. McLaughlin, C. and Davidson, D. *Spiritual Politics,* Findhorn, 1994.
2. Bailey, A. *A Treatise on White Magic*, Lucis Trust, New York, 1998.
   Page, C. *The Frontiers of Health* 1996.
3. Blatzer, J.P. *The Donning International Encyclopaedic Psychic Dictionary*, The Donning Company, 1986.
4. Newton, M. *Destiny of Souls*, Llewellyn, 2000.

5. Powell, A. E. *The Astral Body*, Kessinger Publishing Co., 1998
   Page, C. *The Frontiers of Health* 1996.
6. Stevenson, I. *Where Reincarnation and Biology Intersect*, Praeger Publishers, 1997.
7. Guirdham, A. *The Cathars and Reincarnation,* Spearman, 1992.
8. Tomlinson, A. *Exploring the Eternal Soul*, O Books, 2007.
9. Rinpoche, S. *The Tibetan Book of Living and Dying,* Rider, 1992.
10. Hopking, A. *The Emergence of the Planetary Heart*, Godshaer Publishing, 1994.
11. Browne, S. *Life on the Otherside – A Psychic's Tour of The Afterlife*, Platkus, 2001.

CHAPTER 3 - STARTING A PAST-LIFE

1. Erickson, M. & Rossi, E. *Hypnotic Realities*, New York, Ivington, 1979.
2. Wolinsky, S. *Trances People Live*, The Bramble Company, 1991.
3. Netherton, M. and Shiffren, N. *Past Lives Therapy.* Morrow, New York, 1979.
4. Woolger, R. *Other Lives Other Selves*, Thorsons, 1999.

CHAPTER 4 - EXPLORING A PAST-LIFE

1. TenDam, H. *Deep Healing*, Tasso Publishing, 1996.

CHAPTER 5 - THE PAST-LIFE DEATH

1. Rinpoche, S. *The Tibetan Book of Living and Dying,* Rider, 1992.
2. Powell, A. E. *The Etheric Double*, Theosophical Press, 1989.

CHAPTER 6 - TRANSFORMATION IN THE SPIRIT REALMS

1. Tomlinson, A. *Exploring the Eternal Soul*, O Books, 2007.

CHAPTER 7 - BETWEEN LIVES SPIRITUAL REGRESSION

1. Newton, M. *Life Between Lives; Hypnotherapy for Spiritual Regression*, Llewellyn, 2004.
2. The Michael Newton Institute, contact website; http://www.newtoninstitute.org.
3. Newton, M. *Journey of Souls*, Llewellyn, 1994.
4. Woolger, R. *Other Lives Other Selves*, Thorsons, 1999.
5. Tomlinson, A. *Exploring the Eternal Soul*, O Books, 2007.
6. Newton, M. *Destiny of Souls*, Llewellyn, 2000.

CHAPTER 8 - WORKING WITH BODY MEMORIES

1. Kurtz, R. *The Body Reveals* Harper, New York, 1976.
2. Reich, W. *Studies in Psychology*, Pearson Custom Pub., 1991.
3. *Deep Memory Process* superseded Dr Roger Woolger original work *Integral Regression Therapy*. It is provided through regular international training programs and workshops together with spirit release, ancestor work, spiritual psychology and related topics. Websites:
   US and Europe: www.rogerwoolger.com.
   Germany, Austria and Switzerland: www.woolger.de.
   Brazil: www.woolger.com.br.
4. Woolger, R. and Tomlinson, A. *Deep Memory Process and the Healing of Trauma*, article published in the Network Review, Journal of the Scientific and Medical Network, Summer 2004.
   Woolger, R. *Healing your Past Lives – Exploring the Many Lives of the Soul*, Sounds True, 2004.
   Woolger, R. *Body Psychotherapy and Regression: the Body Remembers Past Lives* in Staunton, T. *Body Psychotherapy*, Routlege, London, 2002.

5. Ogden, P. Minton, K. *Sensorimotor Psychotherapy: One Method for Processing Traumatic Memory,* Traumatology, 6(3), Article 3, October 2000.
6. Staunton, T. *Body Psychotherapy*, Routlege, London, 2002.
7. Greenberg, E. and Woolger, R. *Matrix Therapy,* available from the author.
8. Givens, A. *The Process of Healing,* Libra Books, San Diego, California, 1991.
9. Herman, J. *Trauma and Recovery,* New York: Basic Books, 1992.
10. Stevens, R. *Understanding the Self,* The Open University, Sage Publications, 1996.

CHAPTER 9 - INTRUSIVE ENERGY

1. Baldwin W. *Spirit Releasement Therapy*, Headline Books, 1995
2. Ireland-Frey, L., *Freeing the Captives,* Hampton Roads Publishing, 1999.
3. Cannon, D, *Between Death and Life: Conversations With a Spirit*, Gateway, 2003.
4. The Spirit Release Foundation, website www.spiritrelease.com
5. Newton, M. *Destiny of Souls*, Llewellyn, 2002.
6. Di Griffiths runs training courses in Intrusive Energy. Email; diana.benjamin@virgin.net.

CHAPTER 10 - INTEGRATION

1. Parks, P. *Rescuing the Inner Child,* Human Horizons Series, 2002.

CHAPTER 11 - THE INTERVIEW

1. Frank, J.D. *Therapeutic Factors in Psychotherapy*, American Journal of Psychotherapy, 25, 1971.
2. Erickson, M.H. Zeigg, J. K. *Symptom Prescription for Expanding the Psychotic's World View,* contained in Dolan, Y. *A Path with a Heart - Ericksonian Utilisation with*

Resistant and Chronic Clients, Brunner Mazel, New York, 1985.
3. Maxmen, J.S., Ward, N. G. *Psychotropic Drugs Fast Facts*, W.W. Norton, 1995.
4. Breggin, P., Cohen, D. *Your Drug May Be Your Problem*, Perseus Books, 1999.

APPENDIX I - NOTES

1. Van der Maesen, R. in *The Journal of Regression Therapy, Volume XII (1), PLT for Giles De La Tourettes's Syndrome* International Association for Regression Research and Therapies, 1998.
2. Van der Maesen, R. in *The Journal of Regression Therapy, Volume XIII (1), Past-Life Therapy for People who Hallucinate Voices* International Association for Regression Research and Therapies, 1999.
3. Fonagy, P., Roth, A. *What Works for Whom*, The Guildford Press, 1996.
4. Snow, C. *Past-Life Therapy: The Experiences of Twenty-Six Therapists,* The Journal of Regression Therapy, Volume I (2), 1986.
5. TenDam, H. *Deep Healing*, Tasso Publishing, 1996.
6. Jung. C.G., Hull, R.F.C. *The Archetypes and the Collective Unconscious,* Routledge, 1991.
7. Assagioli, R.M.D. *Psychosynthesis: A Manual of Principles and Techniques,* Aquarian Press 1990.
8. Boorstein, S. (ed.), *Transpersonal Psychotherapy.* Suny, 1996.
9. Dolan, Y. *A Path with a Heart - Ericksonian Utilization with Resistant and Chronic Clients*, Brunner Mazel, New York, 1985.
10. Dilts, R. *Beliefs*, Metamorphous Press, Oregon, 1993
11. Tomkins, P., Lawley, J. *Metaphors in Mind, Transformation through Symbolic Modeling*, The Developing Company, 2000
12. Nolte, J. *Catharsis From Aristotle to Moreno* Action Methods Training Center, Indianapolis, 1992.
13. Wilkins, P. *Psychodrama (Creative Therapies in Practice),* Sage Publications Ltd, 1999.

14. Van der Kolk, B. McFarland and Weisaeth (eds) *Traumatic Stress,* Guildford Press, New York, 1996.
15. MacLean, P. D. *Brain evolution relating to family, play, and the separation call,* Archives of General Psychiatry, 42, 405-417, 1985.
16. Bailey, A. *Esoteric Healing.* Lucis Trust, New York, 1999.
    Powell, A. E. *The Astral Body*, Kessinger Publishing Co., 1998.
    Powell, A. E. *The Etheric Double*, Theosophical Press, 1989.
17. Woolger, R. *Past-Life Therapy, Trauma Release and the Body* available from the author.

APPENDIX III - STRUCTURING A SPIRITUAL REGRESSION SESSION

1. Newton, M *Life Between Lives; Hypnotherapy for Spiritual Regression*, Llewellyn, 2004.

BIBLIOGRAPHY

Assagioli, R.M.D. Psychosynthesis: *A Manual of Principles and Techniques*, Aquarian Press, 1990.

Bailey, A. *A Treatise on White Magic*, Lucis Trust, New York, 1998.

Bailey, A. *Esoteric Healing*, Lucis Trust, New York, 1999.

Baldwin, W. *Spirit Releasement Therapy*, Headline Books, 1995.

Blatzer, J.P. *The Donning International Encyclopedic Psychic Dictionary*, The Donning Company, 1986.

Boorstein, S. (ed.) *Transpersonal Psychotherapy*, Suny, 1996.

Bowlby, J. *The Making and Breaking of Affectional Bonds*, Roultledge, 1994.

Bowman, C. *Children's Past Lives*, Element, 1998.

Breggin, P., Cohen, D. *Your Drug May Be Your Problem*, Perseus Books, 1999.

Brennan, B. *Hands of Light*, Bantam, 1988.

Browne, S. *Life on the Otherside – A Psychic's Tour of The Afterlife*, Platkus, 2001.

Collins, M. *The Idyll of the White Lotus,* Theosophical Books.

Cannon, D, *Between Death and Life: Conversations With a Spirit*, Gateway, 2003.

Crasilneck, H.B. & Hall, J.A. *Clinical Hypnosis Principals and Applications*, Grune & Stratton, 1985.

Daily Mail, Dec 14th 2001, page 11.

Dilts, R. *Beliefs*, Metamorphous Press, Oregon, 1993.

Dolan, Y. *A Path with a Heart - Ericksonian Utilization with Resistant and Chronic Clients*, Brunner Mazel, New York, 1985.

Dychtwald, K. *Body-Mind*, Pantheon, New York, 1986.

Erickson, M. & Rossi, E. *Hypnotic Realities*, New York, Ivington, 1979.

Erickson, M.H., Zeigg, J. K. *Symptom Prescription for Expanding the Psychotic's World View,* in Rossi, E.L. *The Collected Papers of Milton H. Erickson*, Vol IV, Ivington.

Fonagy, P., Roth, A. *What Works for Whom*, The Guildford Press, 1996.

Frank, J.D. *Therapeutic Factors in Psychotherapy*, American Journal of Psychotherapy, 25, 1971.

Gallup, G. *A Look Beyond the Threshold of Death*, London Souvenir, 1983.

Givens, A. *The Process of Healing,* Libra Books, San Diego, California, 1991.

Greenberg, E. and Woolger, R. *Matrix Therapy* available from the author.

Grof. S. *Beyond the Brain*, New York; State University, 1985.

Guirdham, A. *The Cathars and Reincarnation*, Spearman, 1992.

Havens, R. and Walters, C. Hypnotherapy Scripts - *A Neo-Erickson Approach to Persuasive Healing*, Brunner Mazel, 1989.

Herman, J. *Trauma and Recovery,* New York: Basic Books, 1992.

Hopking, A. *The Emergence of the Planetary Heart*, Godshaer Publishing, 1994.

Ireland-Frey, L. *Freeing the Captives,* Hampton Roads Publishing, 1999.

Jung, C.G., Hull, R.F.C. *The Archetypes and the Collective Unconscious,* Routledge, 1991.

Krippner, S., Rubin, R. *Galaxies of Life; the Human Aura in Acupuncture and Kirlian Photography*, Gordon and Beach, New York, 1974.

Kurtz, R. *The Body Reveals,* Harper, New York, 1976.

Lawton, I. *The Book of the Soul*, Rational Spiritual Press, obtainable from website; http://www.rspress.org, 2004.

Lawton, I. *Wisdom of the Soul*, Rational Spiritual Press, obtainable from website; http://www.rspress.org, 2006.

Levine, P. *Waking the Tiger: Healing Trauma.* Berkeley, CA: North Atlantic Books, 1997.

Lucas, W. (ed.) *Regression Therapy: A Handbook for Professionals.* Vol 1. Deep Forest Press, 1993.

MacLean, P. D. *Brain Evolution Relating to Family, Play, and the Separation Call,* Archives of General Psychiatry, 42, 405-417, 1985.

Maj, M., Sartorius, N., Okasha, A., Zohar, J., *Obsessive Compulsion Disorder*, Wiley, 2000.

Maxmen, J.S., Ward, N. G. *Psychotropic Drugs Fast Facts*, Norton, 1995.

McLaughlin, C. and Davidson, D. *Spiritual Politics,* Findhorn, 1994.

Mead, G.R.S. *The Doctrine of the Subtle Body in Western Tradition*, Society of Metaphysics, 1987.

Michael Newton Institute, *Training Manual*, contact website; http://www.newtoninstitute.org.

Netherton, M. and Shiffren, N. *Past Lives Therapy,* Morrow, New York, 1979.

Newton, M. *Destiny of Souls*, Llewellyn, 2000.

Newton, M. *Journey of Souls*, Llewellyn, 1994.

Newton, M *Life Between Lives; Hypnotherapy for Spiritual Regression*, Llewellyn, 2004.

Nolte, J. *Catharsis From Aristotle to Moreno,* Action Methods Training Center, Indianapolis, 1992.

Ogden, P. Minton, K. *Sensorimotor Psychotherapy: One Method for Processing Traumatic Memory,* Traumatology, 6(3), Article 3, October 2000.

Oschman, J. L. *Energy Medicine: The Scientific Basis*, Churchill Livingstone, 1999.

Page, C. *The Frontiers of Health,* 1996.

Parks, P. *Rescuing the Inner Child,* Human Horizons Series, 2002.

Perls, F., Hefferline, R., Goodman, P. *Gestalt Therapy*, The Gestalt Journal Press, 1994.

Powell, A. E. *The Astral Body*, Kessinger Publishing Co., 1998.

Powell, A. E. *The Etheric Double*, Theosophical Press, 1989.

Praagh, J. *Talking to Heaven, A Mediums Message of Life After Death*, Piatkus, 1997.

Reich, W. *Studies in Psychology*, Pearson Custom Pub., 1991.

Rinpoche, S. *The Tibetan Book of Living and Dying,* Rider, 1992.

Rossi, E., Cheek, B. *Mind Body Therapy*, Norton, 1994.

Rumi, *These Branching Moments*, versions by Coleman Barks, Copper Beech, 1988.

Rycoft, C. *Reich,* Fontana Paperback, 1971.

Snow, C. *Past-Life Therapy: The Experiences of Twenty-Six Therapists,* The Journal of Regression Therapy, Volume I (2), 1986

Some, P.M. *Of Water and Spirit – Ritual, Magic in the Life of an African Shaman*, Penguin, 1994.

Stevens, R. *Understanding the Self,* The Open University, Sage Publications, 1996.

Stevenson, I. *Where Reincarnation and Biology Intersect*, Praeger Publishers, 1997.

Stevenson, I. *Twenty cases of Suggested Reincarnation*, University, 1995.

TenDam, H. *Deep Healing*, Tasso Publishing, 1996.
Ten Dam, H. *Exploring Reincarnation*, Tasso Publishing, 1987.
Tomkins, P., Lawley, J. *Metaphors in Mind, Transformation through Symbolic Modeling*, The Developing Company, 2000.
Tomlinson, A. *Exploring the Eternal Soul*, O Books, 2007.
Van der Kolk, B. McFarland and Weisaeth (eds) *Traumatic Stress* Guildford Press, New York, 1996.
Van der Kolk, B. *The Compulsion to Repeat the Trauma: Re-enactment, Revictimization, and Masochism.* This article first appeared in Psychiatric Clinics of North America, 12, (2), 389-411, 1989.
Van der Maesen, R. in *The Journal of Regression Therapy, Volume XII (1), PLT for Giles De La Tourettes's Syndrome,* International Association for Regression Research and Therapies, 1998.
Van der Maesen, R. in *The Journal of Regression Therapy, Volume XIII (1), Past-Life Therapy for People who Hallucinate Voices,* International Association for Regression Research and Therapies, 1999.
Van Lommel, P. et al, *Near-death Experience in Survivors of Cardiac Arrest*; a prospective study in the Netherlands, The Lancet, 15 Dec 2001; Anonymous teeth case.
Van Wilson, D. *The Presence of Other Worlds,* Harper Row, 1975.
Weiss, B. *Many Lives, Many Masters*, Simon and Schuster, 1988.
Wilbarger, P., Wilbarger, J. (1997) *Sensory defensiveness and related social/emotional and neurological problems,* Van Nuys, CA: Wilbarger, obtained from Avanti Education Program, 14547 Titus St., Suite 109, Van Nuys, CA, 91402.
Wilkins, P. *Psychodrama - Creative Therapies in Practice,* Sage Publications Ltd, 1999.
Wirth, D. P. *The Effect of Non-contact Therapeutic Touch on the Healing Rate of Full Thickness Dermal Wounds,* Journal of Subtle Energies & Energy Medicine, Vol. 1 No. 1,1990.
Wolinsky, S. *Trances People Live*, The Bramble Company, 1991.
Woolger, R. *Other Lives Other Selves*, Thorsons, 1999.
Woolger, R. *Healing your Past Lives – Exploring the many Lives of the Soul*, Sounds True, 2004.
Woolger, R. *Past-Life Therapy, Trauma Release and the Body* available from the author.

Woolger, R. and Tomlinson, A. *Deep Memory Process and the Healing of Trauma,* article published in the *Network Review*, Journal of the Scientific and Medical Network, Summer 2004.

ABOUT THE AUTHOR

Andy Tomlinson is a psychology graduate and registered UK psychotherapist. He has been trained in Eriksonian hypnotherapy and regression therapy, and is an International Board of Regression Therapy certified past-life therapist. He is also a certified Life between Lives therapist with the Michael Newton Institute. Andy has run an internationally renowned private practice dedicated to regression therapy since 1996. He is currently the Director of Training for the Past Life Regression Academy, and a founder member of the European Academy of Regression Therapy. This is a group of European regression therapy organizations that work to the same quality standards. He is also a founding member of the European Association of Regression Therapy. He trains, lectures and gives talks internationally on past lives and the soul memories between them. For further information about Andy or his training see *www.regressionacademy.com.*

INDEX

Woolger, R. and Tomlinson, A. *Deep Memory Process and the Healing of Trauma*, article published in the *Network Review*, Journal of the Scientific and Medical Network, Summer 2004.

ABOUT THE AUTHOR

Andy Tomlinson is a psychology graduate and registered UK psychotherapist. He has been trained in Eriksonian hypnotherapy and regression therapy, and is an International Board of Regression Therapy certified past-life therapist. He is also a certified Life between Lives therapist with the Michael Newton Institute. Andy has run an internationally renowned private practice dedicated to regression therapy since 1996. He is currently the Director of Training for the Past Life Regression Academy, and a founder member of the European Academy of Regression Therapy. This is a group of European regression therapy organizations that work to the same quality standards. He is also a founding member of the European Association of Regression Therapy. He trains, lectures and gives talks internationally on past lives and the soul memories between them. For further information about Andy or his training see *www.regressionacademy.com.*

INDEX